THE

SEVEN AGES OF WASHINGTON

Houdon's Statue of Washington at Richmond, Va.

The Seven Ages of Washington

A BIOGRAPHY
by OWEN WISTER
Illustrated

GROSSET & DUNLAP, *Publishers*
by arrangement with The Macmillan Company

TO
S. B. W.
FROM
HER SON

PREFACE

To an invitation from the University of Pennsylvania
this book is due. The Washington orator chosen for 1907
found himself at a late hour compelled to renounce his
task, and this honor fell from him upon me. Saving its
scheme, little of the speech remains; English meant for
the ear of an audience differs in fibre from English meant
for the eye of a reader; besides this, the limit of an
address shuts out much that belongs to the subject. I
had hoped to write this book short enough to be read in
one comfortable sitting; such brevity has proved beyond
my skill. I have attempted a full-length portrait of
Washington, with enough of his times to see him clearly
against; for this, his own writings, so admirably edited
by Mr. Worthington Chauncey Ford in fourteen volumes,
are the material. My other authorities are noted in a
table at the end. Certain anecdotes, not before given
to the public, are due to the kindness of friends and to
some privately published memoirs. Many things that
must have been in his letters to his wife, discreetly de-
stroyed, we shall never know.

Philadelphia, October 20, 1907.

CONTENTS

LIST OF ILLUSTRATIONS

THE SEVEN AGES OF WASHINGTON

On the 22d of February, 1792, Congress was sitting in Philadelphia, and to many came the impulse to congratulate the President upon this, his sixty-first birthday; therefore a motion was made to adjourn for half an hour, that this civility might be paid. The motion was bitterly opposed, as smacking of idolatry and as leaning toward monarchy. Then it was the eighteenth century, it is the twentieth now; but when the 22d of February comes, the United States of America adjourn for a day to honor the memory of George Washington.

At the present time it is odd to recognize that what did come to suffer by the idolatry so much feared by Congress, was not our republic, but the natural, manly, and human character of Washington in the hands of his early biographers. What was done, for instance, to his letters in the generation of our grandfathers, we grandsons would refuse to believe, were we merely told such a story; but to-day we can look at the original letters with our own eyes, and see the strange tricks that were played with them by their first editor.

Washington wrote: "Our rascally privateersmen go on at the old rate;" "rascally" was taken out in the printing as a word indecorous for the father of his country to be seen using.

In another place: "Such a dearth of spirit pray God I may never witness again," becomes, "Such a dearth of spirit pray God's mercy I may never witness again."

In still a third (the subject is a contemplated appropriation): "One hundred thousand dollars will be but a flea-bite," is changed to, "one hundred thousand dollars will be totally inadequate."

By such devices was a frozen image of George Washington held up for Americans to admire, rigid with congealed virtue, ungenial, unreal, to whom from our school-days up we have been paying a sincere and respectful regard, but a regard without interest, sympathy, heart — or indeed, belief. It thrills a true American to the marrow to learn at last that this far-off figure, this George Washington, this man of patriotic splendor, the captain and savior of our Revolution, the self-sacrificing, devoted President, was a man also with a hearty laugh, with a love of the theatre, with a white-hot temper, who when roused could (for example) declare of Edmund Randolph: "A damneder scoundrel God Almighty never permitted to disgrace humanity."

The unfreezing of Washington was begun by Irving, but was in that day a venture so new and startling that Irving, gentleman and scholar, went at it gingerly and with many inferential deprecations. His hand, however, first broke the ice, and to-day we can see the live and human Washington, full length. He does not lose an inch by it, and we gain a progenitor of flesh and blood.

Between all great men there is one signal family likeness; so much is in them, such volume and variety, that by choosing this and leaving out that, portraits almost conflicting could be made of the same character, each based wholly upon fact, yet not all the facts, and so a false picture of the man. From Julius Cæsar could be drawn a profligate and fashionable idler, rather vain of the verses which it was his desultory pleasure to compose. Out of Napoleon could be made a beneficent law-giver, warmly concerned with questions of education. To read the several journals that Washington wrote at Mount Vernon, you would scarce guess that public life engaged a moment of his thought, or that he had ever seen a day's fighting. The hints of greatness in those pages are a huge energy, and a grasp of detail, a memory and attention for the smallest as well as the largest things, that leave one silent with wonder. But no direct sign of the soldier or statesman is there; the writer is apparently a breeder of horses, dogs, and sheep, a planter of trees and crops, generous to his relations and relations-in-law, with his slaves both humane and strict, most strict in his business duties to others, and in their business duties to him. He is also a constant sportsman, fox-hunter, and host, who is pleased to bid many welcome at his table, but dearly likes chosen friends to come in; and with these he takes a more familiar glass of Madeira. To the matter of wine he gives the same measured, minute attention that he gives to his fields, his horses, his rams, and all else. Twice he writes explicit directions about it, the second

5

being as follows, in 1794, when his duties as President keep him absent from home:—

"In a letter from Mrs. Fanny Washington . . . she mentions, that since I left Mount Vernon she has given out four dozen and eight bottles of wine . . . I am led by it to observe, that it is not my intention that it should be given to every one who may incline to make a convenience of the house in travelling, or who may be induced to visit it from motives of curiosity. There are but three descriptions of people to whom I think it ought to be given: first, my *particular* and intimate acquaintance, in case business should call them there, such for instance as Doctor Craik, 2dly, some of the *most* respectable foreigners who may, perchance, be in Alexandria or the federal city; and be either brought down, or introduced by letter, from some of my particular acquaintance as before mentioned; or thirdly, to persons of some distinction (such as mem-

6

bers of Congress, &c.) who may be travelling through the country from North to South, or from South to North . . . Unless some caution of this sort governs, I should be run to an expense as improper as it would be considerable; — for the duty upon Madeira wine makes it one of the most expensive liquors that is now used, while my stock of it is small, and old wine (of which that is) is not to be had upon any terms: for which reason, and for the limited purposes already mentioned, I had rather you would provide claret, or other wine on which the duty is not so high, than to use my Madeira, unless it be on very extraordinary occasions. I have no objection to any sober, or orderly person's gratifying their curiosity in viewing the buildings, gardens, &c., about Mt. Vernon; but it is only to such persons as I have described that I ought to be run to any expense on account of these visits of curiosity, beyond common civility and hospitality.

7

No gentleman who has a proper respect for his own character (except relations and intimates) would use the house in my absence for the sake of conveniency. . . ."

Such orders are given about every item of his domestic and agricultural establishment, and this all through a period when his mind was deep in public matters of a most vexing and delicate kind, both at home and abroad; when he was writing long letters to Hamilton, to Jay, to Adams, to Congress, about our threatened relations with England, and the Pennsylvania Whiskey Rebellion. Nor were these letters dictated — they were in addition to those dictated; nor yet were they thin or of hasty judgment; they were as thorough as what he writes about his wine; and this radiation of energy and sagacity began with him before he was twenty, and continued during some forty-seven years until his death. Not seldom, in reading Washington's correspondence, one pauses simply to

8

dwell upon the marvel of how such power for work ever got itself into one human body. He judged himself well (his judgment was seldom wrong about anything) when in early life he wrote Governor Dinwiddie: "I have a constitution hardy enough to encounter and undergo the most severe trials, and I flatter myself resolution to face what any man dares."

With the many documents now come to light and a proper study and use of these, there could be readily made (if but words were painters' brushes and facts were colors) a gallery of portraits, each of Washington, and all faithful likenesses. His schoolboy face might then be seen, and how he looked in adolescence, when he was surveying for Lord Fairfax, and between whiles making love so precocious, continued, and apparently barren of reward. That older face which Stuart has given us, weather-beaten, warbeaten, deeply toned with retrospect, tells not of those far early Virginia days. And in truth, to sum up a man as he ends, or as he begins, or at any single hour of his life, is to present but a fragment of him; for he is ceasing to be some things, while he is beginning to be other things; and it is all a ceasing, and a beginning, and an overlapping. Who could tell in August what the fruit tree was in May?

In the October of his days, Washington writes from Mt. Vernon: "The more I am acquainted with agricultural affairs, the better I am pleased with them." And in the November of his days: "To make and sell a little flour . . . and to amuse myself in . . . rural pursuits, will constitute my employment . . . If also I could now and then meet the friends I esteem, it would fill the measure . . . ." Thus the Autumnal Washington; but when he was only April-old, he wrote: "My feelings are strongly bent to arms." And again: "I heard the

10

bullets whistle, and, believe me, there is something charming in the sound." In later years, he remarked, "If I said so, it was when I was young." The man himself had forgotten an earlier aspect of himself. Little, then, shall others understand of him who know only Washington the General, or Washington the President.

Life plants no new seeds in a man, but the sun and the snow of the years both quicken and kill what seeds were in him at his birth, and thus the main trunk of character slowly grows. No more than Rome was the Commander-in-Chief of our Revolution built in a day; to stand that strain required beams and rafters of long seasoning, and if ever a character got long seasoning, it was George Washington's. To survey his sixty-seven years, it seems as if so much had never happened to any other man; certainly no American's life has been more crowded with extreme events — action and reflection galloping

abreast through cities and wildernesses, battles and councils, dealing with a motley
throng of foreign noblemen, native neigh-
bors, wrangling statesmen, starving soldiers,
Indian chiefs, and negro slaves.

"If I said that bullets had a charming
sound, it was when I was young." Yes,
when he was young; before the pitiful
slaughter at Long Island, where he wrung his
hands, saying, "Good God, what brave
fellows I must this day lose;" and before
he had learned to love the sound of the wind
in his trees at Mount Vernon — in short before the sun and snow had much beaten upon
him, and while the beams and rafters were still
unseasoned. Therefore, to draw as near
him as we may across Time's wide silence,
let our eyes travel back through the battles
and councils, the foreign noblemen and
starving soldiers, to his beginning.

I. ANCESTRY

WHEN we look among George Washington's forefathers — which somewhat late re-
search has made easy, though it has not
cleared every point — we see that he was
like them, carried on their deeds and natures
in himself, was less a surprise and departure
in the family type than many a famous man
has been; and this because his greatness lay
in character. It is when genius steps in to
procreation that the bird is of unaccountable
feather, as in the case of Shakespeare. But
we find Washington plain enough in his
English ancestors. He came of good blood,
county blood, blood that had fought and
flowed for its king, had preached for its
king, had been to college, that, in short,
knew something of wars and something of
books; that was allied with other good blood

of England, not the greatest, nor yet the least; that bore a coat-of-arms, which, untranslated from its quaint language, reads thus: Argent, two bars and in chief three mullets Gules. And among those who graced this coat-of-arms we find soldiers, knighted for gallantry in battle, and a preacher, who for sticking to his principles got into much trouble with the Roundheads.

So there stand the ancestors: some with swords and some in gowns; behind them, the fields of England with battle smoke and fair towers, and the painted shields of heraldry.

Such was the boy's ancestral stuff, from such loins did he spring, through an emigrant great-grandfather known in Virginia as Colonel John Washington, a public man, a man of circumstance. His seed did not fall away; the family held its high position, so that seventy-six years after the emigrant's coming, came his great-grandson George into a world where an established place, a re-

SULGRAVE MANOR HOUSE
The Ancestral Home of the Washingtons

spected name, and important friends were his inheritance at birth. With him, a good environment took up and fostered a good heredity: the happiest condition that can befall a new-born creature. Once on his legs, and his own master, the boy made himself worthy of his advantages, and coming from something, became more, — unlike much present-day American youth, who, coming from something, are nothing. But let us carefully remember that George Washington's advantages were no disadvantage to him; it is not ill to dwell on this. There is no harm in going from the tow-path to the White House; the point is, what you do when you get there. Spread-eagle eloquence is apt to proclaim somewhat lopsided generalizations on this head, as if obscurity and poverty were virtues in themselves, and good descent and good up-bringing were crimes. There is nothing in all that, save hurtful imbecility; the truth being, that it is not bad to come

17

from silk purses unless you turn out a sow's
ear yourself, nor yet bad to come from sow's
ears if you turn into a silk purse yourself;
but it would be a pity if the sow's ear became the symbol of our Republic.

Let it be once more said (for it is of great
interest, and has been by historians and
biographers but scantily dwelt upon) that
Washington was no meteoric phenomenon
falling into a family unheralded from the sky,
but very much the reverse, a consistent con-
tinuance of the family pattern, precisely the
kind of crop (only greater in size) to be
expected from former harvests; soldiers
who are knighted for valor, preachers who
stick to their principles, come what may, —
are not such precedents the very elements
and fibre of George Washington? He was
their obvious, proper child, moulded large
at birth; and into his strong grasp was put a
great opportunity. In this coincidence lies
the simple explanation of the man.

II. THE BOY

II

In 1657 began the American Washingtons, when two brothers, John and Lawrence, came to Virginia and established themselves between the Potomac and Rappahannock rivers, by Pope's creek. John became Colonel John in wars against the Indians, as, through similar wars in his turn, did his great-grandson George become Colonel George. In 1694 was born Augustine Washington, who became Captain Augustine, and was twice married. To him by his second venture (as he styles Mary Ball in his will) was born George at the family homestead in Westmoreland county, on February 11, 1731, O. S., or February 22, 1732, by our present calendar. The child's earliest associations, however, were not here, but with the spot of

21

his dearest and latest; for his parents, before he could form memories, had gone to live at their farm on the Potomac. Some ten years later the house, as we partly know it to-day, was built by George's elder half-brother Lawrence, whose inheritance it was, and who named it Mount Vernon from Admiral Vernon, with whom he had served as an officer at Carthagena. When the boy was eleven, Augustine his father died, and he went back to his birthplace, "Wakefield," where he lived with his half-brother Augustine until he was thirteen, going then to live with his mother near Fredericksburg. In these young days, when he and his mother lived in straitened circumstances (the bulk of the estate being left to his half-brothers), Mary Washington seems to have been a very admirable, if not intellectual, parent for her son, beginning well the training of his character. In later days, her change of disposition and her conduct regarding money caused him pain and mortification. In certain of his letters to her, always beginning "Honored Madam" according to the custom of their time, the language contains (and not wholly conceals) the struggle between the man's displeasure and the son's natural respect and affection. Some of their paragraphs make distressing reading, and we turn away, leaving them unquoted.

No more than about the boy's ancestors need we make any guesses about the boy. Though myths of which he is the hero are plentiful, and facts are few, these facts are strong in vividness and go far to drawing a distinct picture of him, and to giving it definite color as well. We had best not make too much, separately, of the rather uncertain legends concerning his deeds of strength, his taming of wild colts, his long throws, his high climbs; he was evidently well muscled from the first — though somewhat lank and hollow chested, and with no

ruddiness of face — and the value of the
legends is not their individual authenticity,
but their united testimony.   Inappropriate
anecdotes about anybody never survive: a
saying attributed to Franklin will be canny,
not dull; a story attributed to Lincoln will
be humorous, not stupid; and it is sure that
Washington as a boy possessed a body strong
and energetic beyond the common, and that
he gave much attention to its exercise.

In children's games he seems to have
shared like any other child, and that he
played soldier and marshalled and drilled
his playmates need scarce be counted a
prophetic sign, even though it was he who
mostly took the part of commander.   He had
seen his half-brother Lawrence making ready
for real wars; to imitate was inevitable, and
military sports have been frequent among
generations of children who never came to
fame either as soldiers or civilians.   If we
are looking for portents thus early, there is

24

SUPPOSED PORTRAIT OF MARY WASHINGTON

something more in the fact that a few years later, at the school in Fredericksburg, when the boy had become perhaps fourteen or fifteen, his schoolmates would come in from the playground with disputes for him to settle. They made the studious boy, solitary with his tasks indoors, their habitual umpire. In such a boy we may warrantably see the father of the man who fifty years later was often umpire between two members of his cabinet, and once wrote: "I have a great, a sincere regard and esteem for you both: and ardently wish that some line could be worked out by which both of you should walk."

But why had the boy with the strong, well-exercised body become solitary indoors at this time? His growing character might possibly have kept him apart, but not indoors, and there is another reason which dispenses with surmise. The means left his mother and her family of five living children was slender, and upon the young shoulders of George, the eldest, had already fallen their burden of providing for himself and for them. One advantage common in that day to the sons of well-to-do Virginians did not fall to him, the eldest of the second family, but to his half-brother Lawrence, the eldest of the first marriage. Lawrence was sent to "finish his education" in England, but George had to renounce the luxury of "finishing" even at home, at William and Mary College, and to make ready by the readiest means to become the support of his mother and her children. Hence the indoor study, hence the solitude, both so marked as to have made an impression handed down by his schoolmate, Lewis Willis. In the manuscript of this gentleman's son, Colonel Byrd Willis, is the following passage about Washington: "My father . . . spoke of the General's industry and assiduity at school as very remarkable. Whilst his brother and other boys at playtime were at bandy and

26

other games, he was behind the door ciphering. But one youthful ebullition is handed down while at that school, and that was romping with one of the largest girls; this was so unusual that it excited no little comment among the other lads."

And now, since portents when they are real are of the deepest significance, we do indeed come upon something worth more than a passing mention. To the boy making ready to support his mother, and denied the "finishing" of college at home or travel in England, fell a timely piece of good fortune: he received the "finishing" from an unexpected quarter; he came under the influence of a civilization more finely civilized than England's, more courteous, more restrained than eighteenth-century England knew.

To anyone familiar with Washington manuscripts, that earliest, the school copy-book of 1745, is well known. In spite of its somewhat damaged state, it reveals faithfully and fully that steadfast indoor ciphering which was to prepare him for supporting his mother. The various formal documents of business and book-keeping appear there, copied slowly in his boyish hand for the sake of securely mastering them, and here and there amid these careful transcriptions, a few scrawled pictures of those he sat in school with, and of birds of uncertain species. But even this evidence of whence began that habit and extraordinary power of method in practical affairs, which later served his country and himself so well, — even this is of secondary interest to the 110 rules of civility, also to be seen in this copy-book of 1745, written with more signs of haste than the transcribed bonds and receipts, as if from dictation. With these rules the boy's strong-built, rough, and passionate nature was deeply instilled before he stepped forth upon his adventurous journey in the world. The part they played in his life — since his public and private acts show their spirit and teaching at every turn—was of the first importance, not to him alone, but also to his country. Moncure D. Conway, who has traced delightfully and admirably the French origin and remarkable history of these rules, says regarding their influence upon Washington's character: "In the hand of that man of strong brain and powerful passions once lay the destiny of the New World, — in a sense, human destiny. But for his possession of the humility and self-discipline underlying his Rules of Civility, the ambitious politicians of the United States might to-day be popularly held to a much lower standard." And to this it should be added, that from these rules and their moulding of Washington's character flowed his power of address — the consideration and the simplicity — which won for him, as it won for no other of his time, the esteem and devotion of those who could help our Revolution in the direst

29

hours of its need. It is scarce worth observing that the coincidence of good seed and
good soil is always necessary, and that if
Washington's character had not been the
field, the rules would have been less fruitful.
But it is well worth observing that they
produced some fruit in two fairly barren
characters: Madison and Monroe were also
taught their good manners, and almost
certainly by these same rules, at the Fredericksburg school, and Madison and Monroe,
when examined close, have little to show but
their courtesy, both being models equally of
urbanity and incompetence.

It was once supposed that Washington
was himself the boy author of these rules;
but they date from 1595 and before his day
had known several translations, imitations,
and plagiarisms, among which was an English
version of 1640 entitled, "Youth's Behaviour,
or Decency in Conversation amongst men.
Composed in French by grave persons for

the Use and benefit of their youth. Now newly translated into English by Francis Hawkins." It is possible, as Mr. Conway shows, that what we find in the copy-book of 1745 was the result of Washington's reading and amending Hawkins by himself. But the amendments seem too skilful for the boy of fourteen, and Mr. Conway's own theory seems almost a proven case. In 1729 there sailed to Virginia with his bride the Rev. James Marye. This gentleman had been educated for the priesthood, and thus must inevitably have met the rules, which were a manual among the religious colleges of France. But he became a Huguenot, and hence an emigrant, settling at first in King William Parish. In 1735 he was called to St. George's, Fredericksburg, where he set up a school, created a large congregation, and died in 1767. To his school went many eminent Virginians, besides those already named, and the good manners of several generations of boys brought James Marye and his school into high respect and reputation, for he taught civility as a branch of education, as he taught arithmetic. As the rules in the copy-book show a correspondence with Hawkins sometimes, but more often with the original French, and as Washington's handwriting here gives signs of haste and correction that do not elsewhere appear, it points to the conclusion that the maxims were dictated to his boys by James Marye, who availed himself, now of Hawkins, and again (and more often) of the original treatise that emanated from the *pensionnaires* of the College of La Flèche in 1595, with the title *Bienséance de la Conversation entre les Hommes*. Let us remember with gratitude and regard the Huguenot emigrant, an exile because of his high principles, who brought these principles to benefit our shores, and became the founder of an honorable family, and the wise teacher of American youth.

For the interest of it, we cite three parallel versions of one of these maxims:—

Washington's copy-book, 20th Rule. "The Gestures of the Body must be Suited to the discourse you are upon."

Hawkins 1. 30. "Let the gestures of the body be agreeable to the matter of thy discourse. For it hath been ever held a solœsime in oratory, to poynt to the Earth, when thou talkest of Heaven."

Original French. "Parmy les discours regardez à mettre vostre corps en belle posture."

Were there space here for all the maxims they should be given, so quaint are they in phrase, so sound in foundation, resting upon the deep moral principle of consideration for others, and many of them applicable without change to modern requirements. But fragments of them must suffice:—

"Be not immodest in urging your Friends to discover a secret."

"Wear not your Cloths foul, unript, or dusty."

"Sleep not when others Speak, Sit not when others stand, Speak not when you should hold your Peace, walk not when others Stop."

"Superfluous Complements and all Affectation of Ceremony are to be avoided, yet where due they are not to be Neglected."

"Read no Letters, Books, or Papers in Company but when there is a Necessity for the doing of it you must ask leave: come not near the Books or Writings of Another so as to read them unless desired . . . look not nigh when another is writing a Letter."

"Speak not of doleful things in a time of mirth."

"Talk not with meat in your mouth."

"Labour to keep alive in your breast that little Spark of Celestial fire called Conscience."

34

Such were the precepts that Washington copied as a boy of fourteen, and they entered like leaven into that young lump of strength. "Your future character and reputation [he writes, forty-three years afterward to a nephew] will depend very much, if not entirely, upon the habits and manners which you contract in the present period of your life." These words are not the facile commonplaces of an elderly man moralizing to a youth; they indicate that Washington was entirely aware of the great influence for good exerted upon his own character by the Rules of Civility. It is a misfortune for all American boys in all our schools to-day, that they should be told the untrue and foolish story of the hatchet and cherry tree, and denied the immense benefit of instruction from George Washington's authentic copy-book.

Ornamental knowledge he had no opportunity for (with life's necessities pressing him so near), and very likely he showed small leaning to it. It is plain that his business bent was already strong in him, and that beyond the necessity, his own instinct chose the line of bonds and receipts, rather than of literature and history. And yet they have been quite wrong who at various times have asserted that he was an ignorant man of but small reading. That he read for practical purposes more than for entertainment is undoubtedly true, and that he held a very humble opinion of his own taste and judgment in literary matters is equally so — yet how interesting is this passage in a letter written to Lafayette in 1788! —

". . . Such are your Antient Bards who are both the priest and door-keepers to the temple of fame. And these, my dear Marquis, are no vulgar functions . . . heroes have made poets, and poets heroes. Alexander the Great is said to have been enraptured with the Poems of Homer. . . . Julius Cæsar is well known to have been a

36

man of highly cultivated understanding and taste. . . . The Augustan Age is proverbial . . . in it the harvest of laurels and bays was wonderfully mingled together. . . . The age of your Louis the fourteenth, which produced a multitude of great poets and great Captains, will never be forgotten; nor will that of Queen Ann . . . for the same cause. . . . Perhaps we shall be found at this moment, not inferior to the rest of the world in the performances of our poets and painters; notwithstanding many of the incitements are wanting which operate powerfully among older nations. For it is generally understood, that excellence in those sister Arts has been the result of easy circumstances, public encouragements and an advanced stage of society. . . . I hardly know how it is that I am drawn thus far in observations on a subject so foreign from those in which we are mostly engaged, farming and politics. . . ."

It is not an ignorant man who writes thus. Somehow at sometime during his life so full of sword and of plough, he had considered the poets and heroes, and the question of subsidized art, although the scanty glimpses that he gives of this consideration make us, who would know him wholly, regret that he was not more often "drawn thus far in observations on a subject so foreign."

At the age of fourteen — the age of the copy-book — he had a wish to enter the navy, which his mother opposed, and he therefore went on with his school and his mathematics, which led him to the study of surveying — a very important fact in his destiny. It was probably now, after his disappointment about the navy, that his home responsibilities grew clear to his conscience and that he absented himself from the playground for the sake of harder study. The girls used to wish that he would talk more; "he was a very bashful young man," is the recorded

38

opinion of one of them in later life; yet Seven Ages of Washington
some girl had already disturbed his dawning
passion. Presently he was writing verses,
though of a quality scarce equal to his mathematics.

"Oh ye Gods why should my Poor resistless Heart
   Stand to oppose thy might and power—
      *   *   *   *   *
"In deluding sleepings let my eyelids close
   That in an enraptured dream I may
In a rapt lulling sleep and gentle repose
   Possess those joys denied by day."

Other lyrics to other ladies are found in his
early writing, but maturer passion ended by
expressing itself in prose.

Such was the boy: of vigorous flesh, of
grave spirit rendered graver by necessity, a
respected umpire of school-ground disputes,
a romantic follower of the fair sex; his hair
was brown, his eye blue gray, not flashing
but steady, and he had a nose that his friends
must have hoped he would grow up to.

39

GEORGE WASHINGTON
From a portrait by C. W. Peale

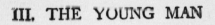

III. THE YOUNG MAN

III

So his schooldays ended, and with them
not indeed his education, for this was just
begun; but schoolmasters and copy-books
were over, and the apron-string was broken.
It was not beneath his mother's roof any
more, but at Mount Vernon, with his brother
Lawrence, that his home was to be. Here
he was to turn his studies in surveying to practical account, and to practical account also
the rules of civility. The working of these in
his character and demeanor brought him that
next experience, that next education, which
may be set among the chief advantages of his
youth. It would seem that the Mount Vernon
neighborhood was poor in gentlefolk compared to Fredericksburg, and that the manners and breeding of this young Washington,

43

who had come here to live, shone out, and won
for him at once the notice of an older man of
high position and noble nature.   Lord Fairfax
lived on his estate adjoining Mount Vernon.
Belvoir, his place (pronounced Beaver),
could be seen from there across Dogue Run,
the little tributary of the Potomac so often
mentioned by Washington in his diaries.   The
boy surveyor — he was not yet quite sixteen
— spent his steady working hours in going
about over his brother Lawrence's lands,
running lines with admirable pains and
accuracy, and his holidays he took in hunting
the fox.   That he relaxed himself between-
whiles sometimes in the composition of verse,
full of the sighs of unrequited love, is less
remarkable at sixteen than the quality of his
surveyor work.   He fell in with Lord Fairfax
while surveying as well as while hunting,
and the nobleman admired the energy which
the lad put into both work and play — but
it may very well be that what endeared the

young surveyor to his lordship was the
gallant manner in which he took his fences.
"Let your recreations be Manfull not Sinfull,"
says Rule 109 in the copy-book. And so
Washington's pluck, and his good, modest
manners, brought Fairfax to make him his
frequent companion in hunting and his guest
at Belvoir, where there were well-bred women,
and Addison's essays, and all was of a piece
of the same sound mellow civilization. In
this good society the boy of sixteen grew
steadily into a man of the world (though of
his bashfulness he never became complete
master, and we shall see this later upon several occasions), and he also learned in farming
and agriculture those standards of English
thoroughness which he endeavored to main-
tain later in the midst of the American
slackness that prevailed then, as it prevails
to-day. What he learned among the ladies
who lived or visited at Belvoir came as nat-
urally to him and was retained as tenaciously

45

by his instinct and his memory as the outdoor knowledge, the planting, harvesting,
fencing, gates, hinges, and all else with which
Lord Fairfax's talk must have abounded,
while the older man and the young rode leis-
urely across country together after a hunt.
Fairfax was bound to comment upon the
slovenly American farming that they passed
by at such times.

Surely his lordship gave the boy a mount
now and then! Surely he sometimes said:
"There's a young horse at Belvoir you had
better try and see if he will do for the ladies."
It is agreeable to think of those huntings;
of the hounds scudding over Virginia's
pleasant hills, and hard behind them the
ruddy-faced nobleman, with George not
quite abreast of him (Rule 57: "In walking
. . . with . . . a man of Great quality, walk
not with him cheek by jowl, but somewhat
behind him") — George therefore keeping
himself a respectful second, controlling the

sinful desires of the spirit to be first — and some love verses forgotten in his pocket. Then in the field corners, by the edges of the covers, stopping to bite a sandwich, surely his lordship would bid the boy come up for a pull at his own flask, and surely the boy, after a proper hesitation, would take the pull! (Rule 40: "Strive not with your superiors in argument.") And so the two ride home, talking together after the hunt; perhaps the boy stops to sup at Belvoir with Lord Fairfax, or perhaps the hunt has taken them to the other side of the country, and Lord Fairfax sups and sleeps at Mount Vernon; and as he and his host, Lawrence Washington, light their bedroom candles, and part for the night, his Lordship says:—

"Your brother's a fine lad, Mr. Washington. We must do something for him, Sir."

And the eyes of the elder brother fill with tenderness and pride at the remark of Lord Fairfax, for he knows it to be true. In the

47

character of the boy he had brought from Fredericksburg, to give a start in life if he could, he had soon discerned a jewel of great price, and his hopes and his love were set upon him.

Next, Lord Fairfax "does something" for young George, makes him surveyor of his great back lands, and the happy boy of sixteen gets on his horse and rides forth to his career. The day is marked in his diary. "Fryday March 11th, 1747–8 Began my Journey in company with George Fairfax, Esqr.; we travell'd this day 40 miles to Mr. George Newels in Prince William County."

That he knew these days for happy ones is not likely, for his nature was not the sort that sits estimating the present moment in reflection, but rather fills it with action; yet in his writings the joy of the new adventure is plain.

"Dear Richard . . . Since you received my letter in October last, I have not sleep'd above three nights or four in a bed, but, after walking a good deal all the day, I lay down before the fire upon a little hay, straw, fodder or bearskin . . . with man, wife and children, like a parcel of dogs and cats; and happy is he who gets the berth nearest the fire."

Only the man that in his youth has known camping, and the joy that comes to him who in many months of the wilderness has not "sleep'd above three nights or four in a bed," can comprehend the delight of life which the young Washington knew at this time. When in afteryears he saw these Fairfax days — the backwoods surveyings and the home-comings to his friend's house — saw this in the far horizon of the past, across the great anxieties, disasters, and triumphs that lay between himself and his youth, it is thus that we find him writing: —

". . . None of which events, however, nor all of them together, have been able to

49

eradicate from my mind the recollection of
those happy moments, the happiest in my
life, which I have enjoyed in your company
. . . and it is matter of sore regret, when I
cast my eyes towards Belvoir, which I often
do, to reflect, the former inhabitants of it,
with whom we lived in such harmony and
friendship, no longer reside there, and that
the ruins can only be viewed as the memento
of former pleasures."

These touching and revealing words were
written from Mount Vernon, May 16, 1798,
after he had been twice President, to Mrs.
Sarah Fairfax in England, where she had
gone to live. She was the widow of that
George Fairfax with whom he began his
surveying journey on that "Fryday" the
11th of March, fifty years before.

He had forgotten the sorrows of that
earlier time, of which the following letter
will give us a smiling glimpse: —

"Dear Friend Robin . . . My place of

residence is at present at his Lordship's, where I might, was my heart disengaged, pass my time very pleasantly as there's a very agreeable young lady lives in the same house. . . . But as that's only adding fuel to fire, it makes me the more uneasy, for by often and inevitably, being in company with her revives my former passion for your Lowland beauty; whereas, was I to live more retired from young women, I might in some measure eliviate my sorrows, by burying the chaste and troublesome passion in the grave of oblivion. . . ."

Buried it was not, at once; on the contrary, the lover orders, with as many careful and exact details as if it were a survey, a highly fashionable coat to be made for him: " . . . on each side six buttonholes . . . the waist from the armpit to the fold to be exactly as long or longer than from thence to the bottom. . . ." This is only a part, less than a third, of his directions about this coat, and does it not read remarkably like a survey?

But coat and all, he did not win his Lowland beauty (whoever she was, for later guesses fit the facts imperfectly), and it is plain that he followed now the most usual and most wholesome course of youth — cured one love-wound by receiving another. The next lady refused him twice, we know, how many more times we do not know; but when this case proved hopeless too, young George again had recourse to the like-cures-like treatment, and not for the last time. With him it would seem to have proved invariably successful.

Why was he so unlucky in these affairs? Why did he so fail to win young women's hearts? He was strong, athletic, tall, a daring rider, his manliness had won the hearts of his brother and Lord Fairfax. What, then, was the matter? It is hard to come at the reason, and very likely there is no one reason. In his favor he had those personal attributes just enumerated, and beyond these, the public mark he was already beginning to make. Appointed public surveyor very soon, at the instance of Lord Fairfax, before he was twenty he had the position of adjutant-general with the rank of Major. These are bright trophies to flourish in the eyes of the fair. But we may be sure that he did not flourish them, that the modesty and respectfulness which so commended him to his elderly patron still always became bashfulness when with a young woman; it is moreover possible that his gravity, his lack of quick light talk, frightened them off when it came to tying themselves to it for life. And last, but least by no means, let us remember his nose. It was a formidable feature — it never ceased to be so — and in these budding days of manhood, it beaked out of that young face in overweening scale. Corresponding to this

nose without, was a character within, huge,
forcible, out of scale with the immature years
and experience of its possessor. Perhaps the
reader has at some time known a friend or
acquaintance who was more symmetrical at
thirty than at twenty, who was slow in growing up to himself. Not a few men are so,
and when a creature of Washington's moral
dimensions comes upon earth, his early
personality is sure to be somewhat ungainly.
Moreover, he is certain to crowd those who
are near him without meaning it, or even
knowing it. With the best of intentions, with
the most real modesty, Washington must
have been not seldom an uncomfortable,
unwieldy companion among those of his
own age. If we think these things over,
we feel that we may understand why the
girls would not have him.

His minute directions about a coat have
been seen above, and this care as to dress
never left him. A proper appearance was

54

one of the many things to which his mind, in due proportion, attended, and almost always with that same precision of detail which he gave to all the multitudinous matters, public and private, that he took up. So it was with the harness for his horses, and his carriage; we can find numerous directions written to England about his wife's clothes! If the Lowland beauty and her several successors had ever the faintest inkling that their suitor would supervise their petticoats and far-thingales, we need speculate no further why they one and all dismissed him. In the general panorama of orders about apparel that mingles with his writings, the most interesting trait of all is the appropriate-ness; as he grows older, he orders more sober garments. At no period, young or old, is it common to find him as unspecific as this:—

"FORT CUMBERLAND, 14 May, 1755.

"DEAR BROTHER:

"As wearing boots is quite the mode, and mine are in a declining state, I must beg the favor of you to procure me a pair that is good and neat."

There is one more word to say about the surveys of this frequent young lover; they suffered no neglect through the preoccupations of his heart. So accurate they were, that to this day they stand unquestioned, wherever found.

What did they for his character? — Sleeping (as he records) in "one thread bear blanket with double its weight of vermin," or lodging "where we had a good dinner . . . wine and Rum punch in plenty, a good Feather Bed with clean sheets," or having "our tent carried quite off with ye wind," or meeting Indians coming from war, who entertain him with a war-dance, jumping "about ye Ring in a most comicle manner." It was the apprenticeship, the seasoning; he was learning the alphabet of Trenton and Valley Forge, personal discomfort was nothing to his body or his mind that loved a pretty coat on the proper occasion. His rides, his camps, his river swimming and rough wandering brought him close to those who were to be his soldiers hereafter, and brought them close to him; he and Virginia learned to know each other. He became a woodsman, a pathfinder, a shrewd judge of wild country and of wild human nature, he wore an Indian hunting shirt — but remained civilized all the while. For Lord Fairfax was always there to come home to from the log-cabins; Lord Fairfax at Belvoir, or at Greenway Court his new place, and Lawrence Washington at Mount Vernon, and their visitors, of good manners and urbane knowledge of the great world — gentlemen and ladies — a society to hold the backwoods surveyor to his standards; and there were the books also, *The Spectator*, and other sound volumes that he evidently read beneath their roofs. Thus, while the wilderness entered into his strong body, many wholesome things entered into his strong brain, and tenaciously stayed there.

To us, because we never saw him, it is wonderful to find him adjutant-general of his district at twenty; that is the age when our present privileged youth is carrying brokers' messages, or stealing signs at college. It was not wonderful to those who did see him —his appointment was made easily. After this, it is less wonderful (since we begin to perceive how large his figure was growing in the community) to find him at twenty-two chosen by the Governor of Virginia to go to the agitated frontier upon a general mission of pacification among the French, the Indians, and the restless colonists. His dear brother Lawrence was now dead, whose health for

some years had been failing. A journey to
the Barbadoes had not brought Lawrence the
strength he had sailed there to seek, while
to George who accompanied him (the only
occasion when Washington was ever absent
from our continent) it had brought small-
pox, of which his face carried the marks all
his life. But young Washington had passed
beyond the need of any protector. He returned from his mission to the Ohio —
Venango, Duquesne, let them here be named
— having come safe through many pitfalls
of Indian treachery, French diplomacy, and
frozen rivers.

"There was no way [he writes] for getting
over but on a Raft; which we set about
with but one poor hatchet. . . . Before we
were half way over we were jammed in the
Ice . . . the Rapidity of the Stream . . .
jerked me out into ten feet of Water." Does
this not seem like the wintry wraith of Trenton, prophetically rising?

59

"Our horses were now so weak . . . and the Baggage so heavy . . . myself and others . . . gave up our Horses for Packs . . . I put myself in an Indian walking dress, and continued with them three Days."

"Queen Aliquippa . . . expressed great concern that we had passed her. . . . I made her a present of a Matchcoat and a Bottle of Rum; which latter was thought much the best present of the Two."

These few lines are from many pages recording that journey; pages of hardihood, caution, and resource, with now and then a slight suggestion of amusement, like Queen Aliquippa and the rum.

Thus Major Washington came out from the backwoods, and into the backwoods was sent again almost at once, but now as Lieutenant-colonel Washington. All Virginia knew now that she had found a man. They wished him to head the troops raised to protect the king's land, but he wrote: "The command of the whole force . . . is a charge too great for my youth and inexperience." "Dear George," was the reply, "I enclose you your commission. God prosper you with it." So he was made second in command, but through the death of his superior officer became first before the campaign was over.

God did prosper him — though not in ways immediately visible — for the alphabet of preparation went on, — the severe alphabet of responsibility, injustice, privation, defeat. These, with hard recruiting, scarce horses, scarce men, and stingy pay, were his next apprenticeship. Washington, a colony Colonel, was paid less than a king's captain, and was moreover looked down upon by the king's captain; it was his first taste of that dull superciliousness in the mother country toward her own flesh and blood across the sea, which ended in the estrangement and loss of that flesh and blood for ever.

"I have not offered," Washington writes Governor Dinwiddie, "to control Captain Mackay in anything . . . but, sir, two commanders are . . . incompatible. . . . He thinks you have not a power to give commissions that will command him . . . that it is not in his power to oblige his men to work upon the road . . . whilst our faithful soldiers are laboriously employed. . . . I am much grieved to find our stores so slow advancing. God knows when we shall be able to do anything for to deserve better of our country."

There we have it vivid after a hundred and fifty years — the English officer nasty to his American superior officer, and the English enlisted man nasty to his fellow-American enlisted man, lounging by and letting him do the dirty, digging work! We need to-day no longer take the stilted, absurd view taught us in our schoolbooks, that England was a "tyrant" and a "despot" to us; the facts

62

will not bear it. Every American every day is suffering ten times the tyranny from trusts and labor-unions that we suffered from England before the Revolution; but between those lines of Washington's letter to Dinwiddie, we catch a flash of that intolerable attitude of the Englishman to the American then, whose exasperating effect really did more to throw the tea into Boston harbor and to write the Declaration of Independence than all the acts of Parliament put together. But how bright does the young Washington shine out in that last burst of fervor, where the little homely turn of grammar seems somehow only to make him the more engaging! "God knows when we shall be able to do anything for to deserve better of our country."

Yes; the alphabet of preparation was going on, was even forming into words; though as compared with Trenton and Valley Forge, those future days when the weight and the

63

fate of a nation were to hang like a millstone about his neck, such words seem of but one syllable. He tasted defeat in this Great Meadows campaign, and perfidy of colleagues, and the ingratitude of Dinwiddie — severe but wholesome flavors for the future loser of Long Island and Brandywine, the future comrade of Gates, Conway, and Charles Lee. Good reason had he likewise to lament his total ignorance of French, since trusting to interpreters led to a number of crooked results, by which his reputation was clouded for a while. So once again he marched back from Venango and Duquesne with his new harvest of experience, meagre supplies, scarce horses, faithless allies, his conduct questioned — and in the end no victory. Yet, when all was sifted clear, he came out of it so honorable and efficient amid the general mismanagement, that the Legislature voted him public thanks. His ups and downs in favor also resemble the days to come, when Congress at one moment was for superseding him, and at the next made him military dictator.   He got at this time, too, an Indian name, as later, by the British, he came to be known as "the Old Fox"; — but by that time he no longer spoke of any place as "a charming field for an encounter," as he spoke of Great Meadows in his unwhetted enthusiasm. It was now that his young blood took joy in the sound of bullets, and that he wrote of his strength: "I have a constitution hardy enough to encounter and undergo the most severe trials." We may be quite sure that enormous enjoyment was constantly his, and that peril and the meeting it salted his many troubles; and also we may suspect it was the mental trials of having his conduct questioned, more than any bodily hardships, that caused the "loss of health" he soon speaks of, — nor was the "loss" a heavy one. It looks as if young Colonel Washington had that impatience of any ailment, so common to men who are almost invariably well, and that he took his present indisposition with undue gravity.

Of English superciliousness and insolence he began to have repeated experiences, the king's officers being the offenders; and it is no surprise to find him thoroughly roused by the mean offer of a nondescript sort of rank, a compromise, carrying no pay — this in the face of the recent vote of thanks for his services in the Great Meadows campaign, where the responsibilities of chief in command had devolved upon him. In answer to such an affront, he writes: "If you think me capable of holding a commission that has neither rank nor emolument annexed to it, you must entertain a very contemptible opinion of my weakness, and believe me to be more empty than the commission itself." So he goes indignant to Mount Vernon (now become his own), but it is not for long. Again, in spite of his mother, he is off to the French

66

and Indian wars, wishing "earnestly to attain some knowledge in the military profession . . . under a gentleman of General Braddock's abilities and experience."

Thus he marches to another encounter with adversity — the worst yet. Again it is the old backwoods trail, again Great Meadows, and again Venango and Duquesne, whose sounding names seem to ring like bells of omen through the time of Washington's apprenticeship. This expedition repeated, in greater dimensions, the trials and lessons of its predecessor; British insolence, British stupidity, with failure and catastrophe as the upshot. Braddock applied to the backwoods, against Indians, just the same methods of warfare he had known in settled communities with travelled roads, against white men, and he by no means thanked Washington for offering suggestions about the habits of Indians, and the trackless character of the country.

It has often been said, and is said still, that Washington had no humor; but this has been pushed too far — to the point, indeed, of attributing to him an eternal gravity of appearance and a stiffness of spirit that never stooped so low as fun. Let us provide him with no trait he does not himself disclose, but neither let us rob him of any. Early in this lamentable Braddock expedition, he writes of an escort of eight men he had with him: "Which eight men were two days assembling, but I believe would not have been as many seconds dispersing if I had been attacked." And about this same time: "I have at last discovered . . . why Mrs. Ward-rope is a greater favorite of Genl. Brad-dock than Mrs. F—. . . . Nothing less, I assure you than a present of delicious cake and potted Woodcocks!" Washington had a sense of fun, could be on occasion sedately jocular, and also (as shall be seen) could be surprised into outbursts of hilarity as violent

as his occasional outbursts of rage. His undoubtedly restricted sense of humor was of
its day, eighteenth century; and a retort of
Goldsmith's to Dr. Johnson, while they were
discussing the doctor's ability to write a
fable about little fish, might fit the Father of
our Country well: "Why, Doctor, you could
never write a fable about little fish, you would
make them talk like whales!"

Upon this expedition Washington added to
his experience of military blundering, civil
incompetence, political jealousy, and starving
commissariat, a very valuable new piece of
knowledge — that British soldiers could run
away. He says: "The dastardly behavior
of the Regular troops (so called) exposed
those who were inclined to do their duty to
almost certain death. . . . I tremble at
the consequence this defeat may have upon
our back settlers." But before the end,
before his own miserable catastrophe and
death, poor British Braddock dropped his

superciliousness, and learned to respect his young Virginia aide. Washington has left words about him both friendly and just.

Once more he was at Mount Vernon, but busy, scraping troops together, after four bullets through his coat and two horses shot under him, with such a record of bravery shining through the clouds of Braddock's misfortune, that a clergyman, in a sermon, preached in Virginia and printed in Philadelphia and London, says: "That heroic youth, Colonel Washington, whom I can not but hope Providence has hitherto preserved in so signal a manner for some important service to his country." How strange seems the petulant complaint of John Adams in after days, that Washington owed his distinction to having married a rich wife! He was now appointed commander-in-chief of all forces in the colony, with 300 pounds compensation for his personal losses and his conduct in the Braddock campaign. His

70

familiar letters at this time speak of severe illness, impaired constitution, and damaged private fortune. "I have been upon the losing order . . . for near two years," he gloomily remarks. But there is evidence, in a letter written to him from the Fairfax house, of some alleviations:—

"DEAR SIR: After thanking Heaven for your safe return I must accuse you of great unkindness in refusing us the pleasure of seeing you this night. . . . If you will not come to us to-morrow morning very early we shall be at Mount Vernon.

> "Sallie Fairfax.
> "Ann Spearing
> "Eliz'th. Dent."

Here was another sort of harvest from the French and Indian wars: four bullets through his coat, and two horses shot under him, atoned for bashfulness somewhat—

perhaps had somewhat cured bashfulness,
and so changed his aspect to the female eye,
that if they could not quite marry him, they
almost would.

Alleviations did not prevent him from
promptly starting reform in the militia laws
to insure more strict instruction; the French
and Indian War still framed the colonies in
from North to South with a band of fire
and death, and presently the young commander of Virginia's forces is riding forth
upon a military mission to Boston, with many
alleviations by the way, as his list of expenses
discloses: "For treating ladies to Micro-
cosm 1.8; loss at cards 8.; for a Hatt . . .
for silver lace . . . for 2 pr. of Gloves . . .
for Cockades . . . for Breeches buckle"
etc., — here are the relaxations of the stately
but convivial young dandy, as he passes
through Philadelphia and New York on his
journey. There are no bullet-holes in those
coats; but an arrow from Cupid seems again

to have made a rent in one of them while he was in New York.

It was, however, still a young bachelor who went from these agreeable distractions back into the bloody Indian wars, where his manly heart was soon moved to its depths by pity. He writes Dinwiddie: "I am too little acquainted, Sir, with pathetic language, to attempt a description of the people's distresses . . . but . . . I would be a willing offering to savage fury, and die by inches to save a people." He continued to taste the superciliousness of "Regular" toward "Provincial" officers (England's dense arrogance was laying up for her a cumulative retribution in the colonial heart), and for the first time he came in for the public servant's inevitable portion of newspaper abuse. This mongrel, heel-snapping breed of injustice nearly cost the colony his services; he declared that nothing but the danger of the times prevented his instant resignation. While recruiting, he had been perforce summary both as to man and horses, and the drunkenness of his soldiers at Winchester had driven him to speak excellent but incautious words of "Tippling House-keepers." This brought a violent unpopularity down upon him; it is at this day most comical to read that they threatened to blow out his brains! Many incidents at this time show that high temper of his to have been shrewdly tried, and to have flashed out now and then, — as, for instance, in these angry sentences: —

"Your favor . . . came to hand. . . . In answer to that part, which relates to Colonel Corbin's gross and infamous reflection on my conduct last Spring, it will be needless, I dare say, to observe further at this time, than that the liberty, which he has been pleased to allow himself in sporting with my character, is little else than a comic entertainment, discovering at once . . . his inviolable love of truth, his unfathomable

74

knowledge, and the masterly strokes of his wisdom in displaying it."

At this time tired with campaigning, he was evidently made ill by worry over Governor Dinwiddie's treacherous hostility toward him; he was obliged to leave his post and go to Mount Vernon to recover his strength. But political treachery and hostility were again excellent things to become inured to, else later, when our country's life depended on him alone, they might have proved too much for his unschooled endurance; nor should there go unmentioned, among the various branches of his education during these years of apprenticeship, a control of temper that would have been less perfect had it been more complete; there are times when it is best a man should let loose his rage.

It was nearly six months before his health allowed him to resume his duties at Richmond, at which time we find another lady in surpasses the power of any language that I possess."

The mind, full of all that has happened to us since that May morning when the young Father of his Country stood in the House of Burgesses at Williamsburg, cannot dwell upon the scene without the heart being affected; Speaker Robinson spoke true. Does history contain, anywhere, a wreath of words more beautiful, which time has only set more surely upon its wearer's head? We leave him standing among the Burgesses, tall with his six-foot three, strong and straight from his campaigns, grown comely and commanding, slender but large-made, a beautiful serene width between his eyes, blushing and trembling because they had praised him to his face.

IV. THE MARRIED MAN

MARTHA WASHINGTON
From a painting by Gilbert Stuart

IV

" MOUNT VERNON, 20 September, 1759.

". . . The Scale of Fortune in America is turned greatly in our favor, and success is become the boon Companion of your Fortunate Generals. . . . I am now, I believe, fixed at this seat with an agreeable Consort for Life. And hope to find more happiness in retirement than I ever experienced amidst a wide and bustling world."

The invalid had prevailed in his courting; he had been married on the 6th of the preceding January to Martha Custis, widow of David Parke Custis, and daughter of John Dandridge. She brought to him and Mount Vernon a considerable fortune, and she made later a gracious and dignified figure as the President's wife. Few of her words or acts

81

are recorded, but her discretion has come down to us. In the mind's eye of the Nation she sits forever, serene and kindly in her white cap and kerchief, our country's first hostess. The gentle haze of legend beneficently keeps her, as she should be, a living but quiet spirit, watching from the soft twilight of her privacy the destinies of the Republic she played her part in founding.

It is no great strain of metaphor to say that Washington had now his first chance to sit down since the days when he had pored over his school copy-book; in very truth it made a sort of pause, a breath-taking, between the backwoods and the Revolution, and he loved it best of all. That phrase about his hoping to find more happiness in retirement than in a wide and bustling world was not an elegant moral sentiment written because it was then the heyday of elegant moral sentiments in epistolary prose. His letters certainly show this prevailing fashion of the time, but far

82

less than those of Jefferson, for example, —
less than almost any one's, — their sentences
generally bearing very directly on some point
of vital public or private necessity. He loved
Mount Vernon; to be there with his garden,
and his crops, and his animals, was his deepest heart's desire, and we do not need his
word for it. Were his writings not full of
the conscious and unconscious delight in it,
and yearning for it, his conduct would be
enough; whenever he can, he is always going
back there, and when public service prevents,
sighs often escape him in familiar letters —
letters that he signs "With affectionate regard, I am always yours" instead of "I
am &c.," or "I am, dear Sir, your most
obedient &c.," or any of those reticent
formulas he more commonly uses. It would
not be ill (in a more elaborate account of him)
to present in gradation the various manners
in which he would close a letter; they reveal
much of him and of the situation, from the

"I am &c.," up to the rare "Yours affection-
ately," passing on the way such occasions as
when an unknown lady has sent him a poem,
or when the political matter is very delicate,
and the person a foreigner of distinction,
when he will say: "It affords an occasion
also of assuring you, that, with sentiments
of the highest esteem and greatest respect,
I have the honor to be, &c."

For a while it was now his lot to be generally at Mount Vernon instead of hurrying
somewhere on a horse with ragged soldiers
behind him; this domestic and pastoral
pause of about six years makes the longest
parenthesis in the rush of his public existence
that he ever knew. Its quiet was the quiet
of deep growth in character. We have seen
that he entered it a large man; he came out
of it a great man, ready for what awaited him.
The process is to us invisible; he never set
down his meditations, and the hairbreadth
steps of increase elude the eye as Spring does

84

in turning to Summer; but evidently he pondered, reached conclusions, ripened much, was but little aware of it, and set no value upon it at all as a matter of any possible interest to others. And certainly he would have resented inquiries of a personal sort as unwarrantable invasions of his privacy. Once in later life, his silence when some of the clergy endeavored to force him to declare his religious views, very plainly told them that he considered their attempt a piece of impertinence. It is singular that he should have been made out a devout churchman by some, and an atheist by others, when his own acts and writings perfectly indicate what he was. He gave up taking the Communion in middle life; he attended church regularly as President, and not at all so when living at Mount Vernon; in dying, he said nothing about religion. His nature was deeply reverent, and his letters so abound in evidences of this that choosing among them is hard: —

85

(1778) "The hand of Providence has been so conspicuous in all this, that he must be worse than an infidel that lacks faith, and more than wicked, that has not gratitude enough to acknowledge his obligations."

(1791) "The great Ruler of events will not permit the happiness of so many millions to be destroyed."

(1792) "But as the All-wise Disposer of events has hitherto watched over my steps, I trust, that, in the important one I may be soon called upon to take, he will mark the course so plainly as that I cannot mistake the way."

(1794) "At disappointments and losses which are the effects of providential acts, I never repine, because I am sure the alwise disposer of events knows better than we do, what is best for us, or what we deserve."

These sentences are intentionally not taken from public papers, or formal letters, where convention might be the reason for their existence, but from letters to friends where nothing of the sort was demanded; they are therefore spontaneous expressions, as is this final one, written at a time of great stress:

(1798) "While I, believing that man was not designed by the all-wise Creator to live for himself alone, prepare for the worst that can happen." These words probably state Washington's creed as nearly and fully as it could be expressed; certainly his deeds square with them fully. Do we count among our public men any who lived less for himself alone?

But in these six years of quiet that he now entered upon at Mount Vernon he was able to follow his inclinations, his private taste, to live for himself while the calm between the end of the French and Indian War and the beginning of the Revolution lasted. He must have enjoyed the absence of some things quite as much as the presence of others — he must, for instance, have basked in the cessation of public criticism. It would be a great blunder to think of him as a man without nerves; he was exceedingly sensitive. This quality, perhaps, does not seem to fit with what he was else: a man of far larger frame than common — his measure after death being six feet three and a half inches — with life-long sporting and outdoor tastes, with a brain that worked by slow firm steps to secure conclusions; a man of moderation in food and drink, though a lover of conviviality, a natural leader, with almost indestructible endurance of body, and completely indestructible endurance of spirit. This is a character we should imagine impervious to carp and cavil, being made of such stern stuff; but it will not do to trust imagination in these matters. It was in their foolish attempt to make of Washington what they imagined he ought to be — edifyingly superhuman — that his early biographers missed making him alive. The man himself, as he

has written himself unwittingly down for
ever in his letters and diaries — chokeful
of vigor, nobility, kindness, public spirit,
now breaking out in a fury at some newspaper attack, and now indulging in sedate
fun (somewhat broad at times) — such a
man is far more edifying than any concocted
figurehead of monotonously calm superiority.
It has already been said that Washington's
ill-health at the close of the French and
Indian wars was more owing to mental
strain over the bad treatment he received at
Governor Dinwiddie's hands than to physical
hardship, and that he entertained thoughts
of resigning which were expelled only by
his sense of patriotic responsibility. When
this was past, he did resign. We have also
seen his trembling and stammering under
the embarrassment of praise in public,
and we shall see later his explosion of rage
at a political cartoon shown him during a
cabinet meeting. During the Revolution,

he had a tiff with Hamilton, and Hamilton went off in a huff; almost at once Washington sent a message of amend to his fiery young subordinate. It was a plain case of impatience on the General's part, and is another instance of his nerves. Jefferson wrote that he was the most sensitive man to criticism that he knew. But better than other men's opinions as to this is what he writes himself. On receiving in December 1795, from the General Assembly of Maryland, a declaration of loyalty and reliance, he responded to the governor: —

"At any time the expression of such a sentiment would have been considered as highly honorable and flattering. At the present, when the voice of malignancy is so high-toned . . . it is peculiarly grateful to my sensibility."

Still more freely does he unveil his heart to a nearer friend in 1796, and this passage is worth a dozen opinions: —

"Having from a variety of reasons (among

which a disinclination to be longer buffeted in the public prints by a set of infamous scribblers) taken my ultimate determination 'to seek the post of honor in a private station,' I regret exceedingly I did not publish my valedictory address the day after the adjournment of Congress. . . . It might have prevented the remarks which, more than probable, will follow a late annunciation — namely, that I delayed it long enough to see that the current was turned against me, before I declared my intention to decline."

We find him, then, at sixty-seven, shrinking from the "infamous scribblers" just as he had done at twenty-seven — sensitive all his life long, in spite of honors won, and the seasoning of struggle and of age. These are the things, these contrasts, these seeming contradictions in character, that strike the flash of life, and let us see across the long dark distance the heart of Washington beating, and the blood surging to his face.

It is fabricated consistency that kills naturalness.

Of his humor, if humor it may be called, some instances have been already given. But if we gather before us all the anecdotes of this humor that record has preserved, and consider them as a whole, they show rather a robust sense of fun, a wholesome power to be amused (and sometimes uproariously amused), than any subtle gift and perception. That Elizabethan roughness in mirth which surges through Shakespeare and which still delights the gallery to-day, in the eighteenth century still delighted the boxes as well, all classes of society taking a pleasure in "horse play," which a certain portion of our community has now outgrown in its decadent ascent from vigor to refinement. Washington seldom said droll things, but enjoyed very heartily the droll things of others. We have the story of his laughter when a young horse proved too much for a boastful rider; of his laughter at something told by a famous army raconteur while the two were crossing the Hudson together; of his laughter at a joke made by a visitor which threw the whole Mount Vernon family into mirth, which a parrot at once imitated, when Washington exclaimed: "Ah, you are a funny fellow. See, even that bird is laughing at you." We have also the account of how he laughed at General Putnam (whom he called Old Put, being fond of him) on an occasion which shall be mentioned later. We have other instances, all showing a power to enjoy what the Shakesperian audience enjoyed in the way of fun; — in short, Washington's laughter may be likened to a big bell that needs a good strong hand to make it sound, and then rings out far over the open fields. The light, quick tinkle of our electric age was not anything that he knew, and perhaps no story about this side of his nature is more vivid than one told in a foot note in the life of

Jeremiah Smith, twice Chief Justice of New Hampshire, and a visitor at Mount Vernon in 1797.

"Judge Marshall and Judge Washington (the General's nephew Bushrod) were on their way to Mount Vernon, attended by a servant who had the charge of a large portmanteau containing their clothes. At their last stopping place there happened to be a Scotch pedlar, with a pack of goods which resembled their portmanteau. The roads were very dusty, and a little before reaching the general's, they, thinking it hardly respectful to present themselves as they were, stopped in a neighboring wood to change their clothes. The colored man got down his portmanteau, and just as they had prepared themselves for the new garments, out flew some fancy soap and various other articles belonging to the pedlar, whose goods had been brought on instead of their own. They were so struck by the consternation of their servant, and the ludicrousness of their own position, being there naked, that they burst into loud and repeated shouts of laughter. Washington, who happened to be out upon his grounds near by, heard the noise, and came to see what might be the occasion of it, when, finding his friends in that strange plight, he was so overcome with laughter, that he actually rolled upon the ground."

Here, then, is an aspect of the Father of his Country that has been sedulously kept from all the generations of those whom the priggish, sickening, cherry-tree invention has turned away from loving him for being like themselves after all, and who have given him, instead of their love, only a perfunctory, uninterested respect.

Judge Marshall saw him roll on the ground, but Judge Marshall nevertheless told a friend within three months of his own death that he was "never free from restraint in Washington's presence — never felt quite at ease, such was Washington's stateliness and dignity."

Dignity and rolling on the ground are not incompatible; Washington's character is one of those rare ones which not only can bear the whole truth, but which gains by the whole truth. Another passage from Jeremiah Smith's life will give, as well and as simply as any of the contemporary memories, a glimpse of Washington the man, the host in his own house. The visitor arrived late in the afternoon —

". . . And received a most cordial welcome from Washington and his lady, the latter 'at this time a squat figure, without any pretension to beauty, but a good motherly sort of woman.' After a cup of excellent tea &c., the evening passed in conversation. There were present, besides the family, a son of Lafayette, and another French gentleman. While they were talking, a servant came into the room and said to Washington,

96

MOUNT VERNON
Residence of Washington

'John would like the newspaper, sir.' He replied, 'You may take it,' but after he had gone out, said, 'he had better mind his work.' He then told Mr. Smith a story of his coachman, a long-tried and faithful man. One very rainy day he was obliged to order his carriage unexpectedly, to go a long distance on business. After getting into it he perceived that there was some delay about starting, and putting his head out, he saw that there was a great bustle among his servants, who were trying to mount the coachman on the box, and with much difficulty, at length succeeded. 'What is the matter?' asked the general. The servants replied, that he was intoxicated; 'whereupon,' said Washington to Mr. Smith, 'I was tempted to say to the man at once, be gone about your business.' But the coachman at that moment turned round and said, 'never fear, massa, I'll drive you safe.' 'And I trusted him,' continued Washington, 'and he never drove me better.'

"At about half past nine, Mr. Smith signified his intention of retiring, when Washington also arose, and taking a lamp, led the way to a most comfortable apartment, in which was a fire brightly blazing. He assured his guest that the fire 'would be perfectly safe,' and intimated that he might 'like to keep his lamp' burning through the night.' In the morning, after breakfast, Mr. Smith took leave, though desired to prolong his visit; and a very urgent invitation was given, that he should 'bring his bride to see them.' Horses were brought to the door, and Washington accompanied him some miles on the way. 'He was always,' said Mr. Smith, 'dignified, and one stood a little in awe of him.'"

"A little in awe;" again that touch, given above by Judge Marshall, and by so many others — in fact, unanimously given. That Judge Marshall, himself a considerable man, should have seen Washington roll on the

ground with laughter, yet after that still
never feel quite at ease in his presence is
wonderfully significant of the majestic figure
that Washington must have become after
bearing our young country on his shoulders
through so many years of its weakness and
need. The truth is, a great man cannot do
great things without in a way growing apart
from his fellows, little as he may desire such
a result. For somewhat the same reason the
sight of a huge flood, or a deep chasm, or a
high mountain, inclines all save stunted
spirits to silence, and personal greatness dis-
tils inevitable constraint, and draws around
itself unknowingly a circle of isolation
that is not without its sadness. In Washington's very last years, we read that during
a dance of young people at Mount Vernon,
he came out of his study to take pleasure in
looking on, when a quiet spread over the
gayety of the party. It was explained that
his presence caused it, and then they saw

that tall, weather-beaten figure go back to his solitude from the lights and the laughter whose brightness he was unwilling to dim.

To the little glimpse of Mount Vernon privacy given by Jeremiah Smith — the servant asking for the newspaper, the tale of the coachman, the host lighting his guest to the room with the brightly burning fire — this further picture is worth selecting from the many that have survived. A visitor, who was afflicted with a heavy cold, lay coughing in his bed, unable to sleep, when he became aware of the looming, night-clad form of Washington approaching his bed-side. Washington was bringing him a bowl of tea which he had got out of his bed to make himself for his guest's relief.

It is likely that Washington's familiar talk with his friends (in those rare moments when they were not all obliged to be debating the gravest possible matters) was not infrequently relieved by touches of that sedately expressed fun which occur now and then in his letters, such as the passage about General Braddock and the potted woodcocks. Indeed, we know that he could be jocular in the very heart of a crisis. On that memorable night of Trenton, in the midst of the icy, dangerous Delaware, he turned to Henry Knox with a rough joke that still lives upon the lips of men. But to men's lips it must be confined; a printed page is not the place for it, any more than a china-shop is the place for a bull, who is an object as excellent in the fields as Washington's speech was excellent on the Delaware, in the presence only of Knox and the boatman. His enjoyment of hunt-dinners, and of those songs and jests which come after them, is well known, and his fondness for theatrical shows, and shows in general, was life-long, as was his pleasure in dancing. He danced during war, as well as in peace, and up to within three years of his death — that is to say, when he was sixty-four years old. Perhaps none of his letters better shows the changing from seriousness to amusement, and back again, than the following to Lafayette:—

"MOUNT VERNON, 10 May, 1786.

"MY DEAR MARQUIS,

". . . It is one of the evils of democratical governments, that the people, not always seeing and frequently misled, must often feel before they can act right; but then evils of this nature seldom fail to work their own cure. It is to be lamented, nevertheless, that the remedies are so slow, and that those who may wish to apply them seasonably are not attended to before they suffer in person, in interest, and in reputation. The discerning part of the community have long seen the necessity of giving adequate powers to Congress for national purposes, and the ignorant and designing must yield

102

to it ere long. . . . The British still occupy our posts to the westward. . . . It is indeed evident to me that they had it in contemplation to do this at the time of the treaty. The expression . . . which respects the evacuation . . . is strongly marked with deception. I have not the smallest doubt, but that every secret engine is continually at work to inflame the Indian mind, with a view to keep it at variance with these States for the purpose of retarding our settlements to the westward, and depriving us of the fur and peltry trade of that country.

"Your assurances, my dear Marquis, respecting the male and female asses, are highly pleasing to me, I shall look for them with much expectation. . . .

"The Jack which I have already received from Spain, in appearance is fine; but his late royal master, tho' past his grand climacteric, cannot be less moved by female allurements than he is; or when prompted can proceed with more deliberation and majestic solemnity to the work of procreation. . . .

". . . Your late purchase of an estate in the colony of Cayenne, with a view of emancipating the slaves on it, is a generous and noble proof of your humanity. Would to God a like spirit would diffuse itself generally into the minds of the people of this country. But I despair of seeing it. Some petitions were presented to the Assembly, at its last session, for the abolition of slavery, but they could scarcely obtain a reading. To set them afloat at once would, I really believe, be productive of much inconvenience and mischief; but by degrees it certainly might, and assuredly ought to be effected; and that too by legislative authority."

The jack received from Spain was named Royal Gift in honor of the King's courtesy and compliment to Washington in waiving the law against sending any of that particular breed out of the country, and the animal was the occasion of several other passages in Washington's letters, similar in spirit to that in which he wrote Lafayette.

The breeding of animals was something to which he much attended, he led all his neighbor planters in discovering that there could be no profit in tobacco, while in foreign ports any flour bearing the brand "George Washington, Mount Vernon," was passed without further inspection, because his honest goods had carried their reputation even over the seas.

With his small book learning, his general leaning to sport and the open air, and his uncertain spelling (even in the letter about his marriage, a part of which begins this chapter, he speaks of London as the great Matrapolis) we meet another flash of contradiction in the discovery that he decidedly liked to write. He plainly relished filling pages with his sentiments and opinions, and that beautiful manuscript of his must have been a quick

operation, which it certainly does not seem
in appearance. Yet this, with his well-nigh
miraculous energy, is the only explanation
of how a man, so occupied in action as he
was, managed to pen literally thousands of
pages with his own hand. There can be no
doubt, when we turn over the fourteen
volumes of his published writings, each of
four hundred fifty pages, and by no means
including the entire product of his pen
(they omit seven hundred and one letters
and addresses published elsewhere), that
quite aside from letters of obligation, George
Washington enjoyed sitting down to paper,
quill, and ink, and that when he once got
under way, he was quite likely to fill the
sheet. Sitting down to other things was less
apt to be so welcome, — sitting for his
portrait, for instance, of which he writes: —

"At first I was . . . as restive under the
operation, as a colt is of the saddle. The
next time I submitted very reluctantly, but

with less flouncing. Now, no drayhorse moves more readily to his thills than I to the painter's chair."

In this diverting account of his own progress toward resignation, we may read either his recognition that as a public man he must submit, or else that he came to enjoy it. However this may be, his sundry contacts with artists — painters, sculptors, and architects when it came to planning the Federal City (as it was called before his name was given to it) — led him to form an opinion of the "irritable race" which he expressed with the same happy unmistakableness that characterizes all his opinions: —

"It is much to be regretted, however common the case is, that men, who possess talents which fit them for peculiar purposes, should almost invariably be under the influence of an untoward disposition, or are sottish, idle, or possessed of some other disqualification, by which they plague all

107

those with whom they are concerned. But I did not expect to have met with such perverseness in Major L'Enfant. . . ." And writing two years after this about another architect, his mind peeps forth again: "Some difficulty arises with respect to Mr. Hallet . . . his feelings should be saved and soothed as much as possible."

No one seems ever to have written letters more natural, more redolent of their writer, than Washington; those of many other eminent men — Jefferson, for example — often subtly betray a sense of being composed; but to read the correspondence of the master of Mount Vernon is gradually to feel one's self in his presence, almost as if the man were sitting there, and this quality is, if possible, more striking still in his domestic journal, from which we give a few foreshortened strokes, in order to paint Mount Vernon life in his own words, written during the early years of his marriage.

"Several of the family were taken with the measels . . . . Hauled the Sein and got some fish, but was near being disappointed of my Boat by means of an oyster man who had lain at my Landing and plagued me a good deal by his disorderly behavior . . . . Mrs. Washington was a good deal better to-day but the oyster man still continuing his Disorderly behavior at my landing, I was obliged in the most preemptory manner to order him and his company away. . . .

"Went to Alexandria and saw my Tobo . . . in very bad order . . . visited my Plantation. Severely reprimanded young Stephens for his insolence. . . . After Breakfast . . . rid out to my Plantns . . . found Stephens hard at work with an ax—very extraordinary this! . . . White Frost . . . two negroes sick . . . ordered them to be blooded . . . Stephens at Winchester. Visited my Plantation and found to my great surprise Stephens constantly at work . . . passing by my Carpenters . . . I found . . . George, Tom, Mike and young Billy, had only hugh'd 120 foot yesterday from 10 o'clock. Sat down therefore, and observed —

"Tom and Mike in a less space than 30 minutes, cleared the bushes . . . visited my plantations before sunrise, and forbid Stephens keeping any horses upon my expense." Stephens, by this time, had probably learned to quake in his shoes. "Went to a ball at Alexandria, where Musick and dancing was the chief entertainment . . . great plenty of bread and butter, some biscuits with tea and coffee, which the drinkers of could not distinguish from hot water sweetened . . . I shall therefore distinguish this ball by the stile and title of the Bread and Butter Ball, . . .

"After several efforts to make a plow . . . was feign to give it up. . . . Mrs. Posy and some young woman, whose name was unknown to anybody in this family, din'd here. . . . Spent the greatest part of the day in

making a new plow of my own invention. . . .
Sat my plow to work and found she answered
very well. . . . A messenger came to inform
me that my Mill was in great danger . . .
got there myself just time enough to give her
a reprieve . . . by wheeling dirt into the place
which the water had work'd."

He took off his coat in this emergency,
and labored with his men, and he probably
did so on many another occasion. Such a
way of not merely owning, but mastering,
his property, brought him to a most thorough
and sagacious knowledge of the soil. It
were easy to overload our narrative with
extracts from the copious pages of his agricultural and domestic notes, and this must not be
done; but to omit these altogether would
cause the reader to miss a direct sight of
Washington the farmer and of his astound-
ing power of detail.

"Harrowed the ground at Muddy Hole,
which had been twice ploughed, for Albany

pease in broad-cast. At Dogue Run began
to sow the remainder of the Siberian wheat
. . . ordered a piece of ground, two acres,
to be ploughed at the Ferry . . . to be drilled
with corn and potatoes between, each ten
feet apart, row from row of the same kind.
Sowed in the Neck . . . next to the eleven
rows of millet, thirty-five rows of the rib-
grass seeds, three feet apart and one foot
asunder in the rows." (This was the 14th
of April, 1792.)

"*Corn.* On rows 10 feet one way, and
18 inches thick single stalks; will yield
as much to the Acre in equal ground, as
at 5 feet each way with two stalks in a
hill; to that Potatoes, Carrots, & Pease
between the drilled Corn, if not exhaustive,
which they are declared not to be, are nearly
a clear profit. . . . Let the hands at the
Mansion House grub *well*, and perfectly
prepare the old clover lot. . . . When I say
grub *well*, I mean that everything, which is

not to remain as trees, should be taken up by the roots . . . for I seriously assure you, that I had rather have *one acre* cleared in this manner, than four in the common mode . . . It is a great and very disagreeable eye-sore to me, as well as a real injury in the loss of labor and the crop (ultimately), and the destruction of scythes, to have foul meadows. . . .

"You will be particularly attentive to my negros in their sickness; and to order every overseer *positively* to be so likewise; for I am sorry to observe that the generality of them view these poor creatures in scarcely any other light than they do a draught horse or ox . . . instead of comforting and nursing them when they lye on a sick bed. . . .

"Doll at the Ferry must be taught to knit, and *made* to do a sufficient day's work of it. . . . Lame Peter, if no body else will, must teach her. . . . Tell house Frank I expect he will lay up a more plenteous store of the black common walnut. . . .

"The deception with respect to the potatoes (210 instead of 418 bushels) is of a piece
with other practices of a similar kind . . . for
to be plain, Alexandria is such a recepticle for
everything that can be filched from the right
owners by either blacks or whites. . . .
Workmen in most countries, I believe, are
necessary plagues; — in this, where entreaties
as well as money must be used to obtain their
work, and keep them to their duty, they
baffle all calculation. . . . If lambs of *any
kind* have been sold . . . it has not only
been done without my consent, but expressly
contrary to my orders. And sure I am, the
money for which they were sold never found
its way into my pockets. . . . And I wish
you would reprehend the overseers severely
for suffering the sheep under their respective
care to get so foul as I saw some when I
was at home. . . . It is impossible for a
sheep to be in a thriving condition when he
is carrying six or eight pounds at his tale. —

114

And how a man who has them entrusted to his care, and must have a sight of this sort every day before his eyes can avoid being struck with the propriety and necessity of easing them of this load, is what I have often wondered at. . . .

"It is to be observed, by the weekly reports, that the sewers make only six shirts a week, and the last week Carolina (without being sick) made only five. Mrs. Washington says their usual task was to make nine with shoulder straps and good sewing. . . .

"Desire Thomas Green to date his reports. . . . I fancy it will puzzle him to make out 508 feet in the twenty four plank there set down. . . . How does your growing wheat look at this time? I hope no appearance of the Hessian fly is among it. . . . In clearing the wood, mark a road by an easy and graduated ascent from the marsh . . . up the hollow which leads into the lot beyond the fallen chestnut . . . and leave the trees standing thick on both sides of it . . . if too thick, they can always be thinned; but, if too thin, there is no remedy but time to retrieve the error. . . .

"Spring Barley . . . has thriven no better with me than Vetches. . . . Of the field Peas of England I have more than once tried, but not with encouragement to proceed. . . . The practice of plowing in Buckwheat twice in a season, as a fertilizer, is not new to me. . . . The cassia charmœcrista, or Eastern shore Bean . . . has obtained a higher reputation than it deserves. . . . I am not surprized that our mode of fencing should be disgusting to a European eye . . . no sort of fencing is more expensive or wasteful of timber. . . .

"I find by the reports that Sam is, in a manner, always returned sick; Doll at the Ferry, and several of the spinners very frequently so, for a week at a stretch; and ditcher Charles often laid up with a lameness. I never wish my people to work when they are really sick . . . but if you do not examine into their complaints, they will lay by when no more ails them than all those who stick to their business. . . . My people . . . will lay up a month, at the end of which no visible change in their countenance, nor the loss of an oz. of flesh is discoverable; and their allowance of provision is going on as if nothing ailed them. . . . What sort of lameness is Dick's . . . and what kind of sickness is Betty Davis's . . . a more lazy, deceitful and impudent huzzy is not to be found in the United States. . . . I am as unwilling to have any person, in my service, forced to work when they are unable, as I am to have them skulk from it, when they are fit for it. . . . Davy's lost lambs carry with them a very suspicious appearance. . . . If some of the nights in which . . . overseers are frolicking . . .

117

were spent in watching the barns, visiting
the negro quarters at unexpected hours, way-
laying the roads, or contriving some device
by which the receivers of stolen goods might
be entrapped . . . it would redound much
more to their own credit . . . than running
about. . . . I . . . give it as a positive
order, that after saying what dog or dogs
shall remain, if any negro presumes under
any pretence whatsoever to preserve, or
bring one into the family, that he shall be
severely punished, and the dog hanged. I
was obliged to adopt this practice whilst
I resided at home . . . for the preservation
of my sheep and hogs; but I observed when
I was at home last, that a new set of dogs
was rearing up, and I intended to have spoke
about them. . . . It is not for any good
purpose negros raise or keep dogs, but to
aid them in their night robberies; for it is
astonishing to see the command under which
their dogs are. . . . The practice of run-

118

ning to stores &c. for everything that is wanting, or thought to be wanting . . . has proved the destruction of many a man. . . . I well know that things must be bought . . . but I know also that expedients may be hit upon, and things (though perhaps not quite so handsome) done within ourselves, that would ease the expenses of my estate very considerably."

These quotations, it will be understood, come from no one passage, but are taken from many, written at widely different dates, sometimes in the form of notes, and sometimes addressed to those in charge of Mount Vernon when its master was obliged to be away attending to the Revolution, or the Constitutional Convention, or the duties of President. What is here given is perhaps a thousandth part of the whole, and as we discern Doll at the Ferry and ditcher Charles, and the superfluous dogs, sitting in the back paths and crossroads of Washington's immortality, we see himself, in neither military nor state dress, but easy in his home riding clothes, passing over his fields at sunrise, watching the Siberian wheat, pointing where a new road should go, where a new tree should rise, and happier in those pastoral hours than his more glorious moments ever beheld him. Upon this side of his life and character we cannot dwell again, save now and then to remind the reader that it lay always in the depths of his heart, no matter what else that "spark of celestial fire called conscience" might be driving him to do in the service of his country; we finish our detailed reference to it, with what he wrote Hamilton at the time he was considering his last speech to Congress.

"It must be obvious to every man, who considers the agriculture of this country, (even in the best improved parts of it) and compares the produce of our lands with those of other countries, no ways superior to them in *natural fertility*, how miserably defective we are in the management of them; and that if we do not fall on a better mode of treating them, how ruinous it will prove to the landed interest. Ages will not produce a systematic change without public attention and encouragement; but a few years more of increased sterility will drive the Inhabitants of the Atlantic states westwardly for support; whereas if they were taught how to improve the old, instead of going in pursuit of new and productive soils, they would make those acres which now scarcely yield them anything, turn out beneficial to themselves — to the Mechanics by supplying them with the staff of life on much cheaper terms — to the Merchants, by increasing their Commerce and exportation — and to the Community generally, by the influx of Wealth resulting therefrom. In a word, it is in my estimation, a great national object, and if stated as fully as the occasion and circumstances will admit, I think it must appear so."

At his death in 1799, plans of crops were found written out for 1800, 1801, 1802, and 1803.

His marriage brought him no children, save those of other people — two step-children, and a succession of nephews, nieces, grand-nephews, and grand nieces, these latter littering his domestic life with the responsibilities which their parents had failed to meet. Their support and rearing were loaded upon him, and strung out over a quarter of a century; some of them lived with him, and he was endlessly paying out money for the others — for their food, their clothes, their education, and sometimes for their debts, as he had likewise done on occasion for their incompetent fathers. "Dear Sir [he writes Samuel Washington, the son of his worthless brother Samuel] I perceive by your letter of the 7th Instant that you are under the same

122

mistake that many others are — in suppos-
ing that I have money always at command.
The case is so much the reverse . . . that I
found it expedient to sell all my lands (near
5000 acres) in Pennsylvania . . . Be assured
there is no practice more dangerous than
that of borrowing money (instance as proof
the case of your father and uncles) . . .
all that I shall require is, that you will
return the net-sum when in your power, without Interest." Many are the letters like this,
beginning with a lecture and ending with a
kindness — and many of the loans were still
unpaid when he died; in his will some are
expressly released. Nor was it his own
blood alone; his wife's relations come in
for his help, and her grandchildren. In
one case we find, "Mrs. Haney should en-
deavor to do what she can for herself — this
is a duty incumbent on every one; but you
must not let her suffer, as she has thrown
herself upon me." — What relation Mrs.

123

Haney was to him, nobody has been able to find! Though the whole of this miscellaneous brood of dependents did not turn out as worthless as some of them did, his unceasing generosity and watchful care may be said to have been really rewarded in the cases only of Bushrod Washington, his nephew, and Nelly Custis, his wife's grand-daughter. To her he was devoted, as his constant gifts, and his letters, show, while of Bushrod he was both proud and fond. But he had a niece Harriot, whose name ends by bringing an expectant smile to the lips whenever one comes to a letter addressed to her or a reference made to her. In her way, she evidently annoyed her uncle as much as did Doll at the Ferry, or the oyster man, and when one finally meets a passage alluding to her conduct, which "I hear with pleasure has given much satisfaction to my sister," the smile becomes laughter. When the various boys fallen upon his hands begin to go to school and to

124

college, the good Washington's letters to
them abound in affectionate wise counsel as
to their work, their play, their dress, their
company, their habits; twice, first to Bushrod
and then to George Steptoe Washington (a
grand-nephew) long afterward, he writes
that he is no stoic to ask too much of young
blood. Not the least touching point in the
many documents which record his relations
with all these young people is to find in his
expense accounts: "The Wayworn traveller,
a song for Miss Custis," and for his young
step-children in his early married life, "10
shillings worth of Toys," "6 little books for
children beginning to read," "A box of Gin-
gerbread Toys & Sugar Images or Comfits."

A passage at the close of one of his letters,
written when he was above sixty (with Mrs.
Washington in good health), gravely speculat-
ing upon the possibility of his marrying again,
is in keeping with his habit of weighing all
contingencies; one of his brothers had five

125

wives, he was Mrs. Washington's second
husband, what if he survived her? He
renounces the hope of children, for, he says,
he would not commit the folly of taking a
young wife, but a partner suitable to his
years. The whole paragraph is a very natural
one, if scarcely romantic, and we may be
certain it would have been little pleasing to
Mrs. Washington. It should not be a matter
of regret to us, but rather one of relief, that
he was childless. The spectacle of a great
man's children and grandchildren is so
seldom edifying, and so often mortifying,
that on the whole it is better none of his
direct blood is among us, and that he stands
alone, with no weeds of posterity clogging
round his feet. There is but one family in
all America whose name forms an un-
broken chain of public service and honor,
from its progenitor to the present day; in
this country the abolition of primogeniture
makes such families well-nigh impossible,

and with the gain achieved by such abolish-
ment goes the loss of hereditary family responsibility to the State, — a loss so far not
balanced by the civic responsibility mani-
fested by the American citizen as a unit.
The life and property of the Englishman
are to-day better protected than the life and
property of the American, and this is owing,
in the last analysis, to a better public opinion
and better legislative efficiency in England.
Many a "younger son" has gone into politics
and parliament, and shone there, because of
this sense of hereditary family duty to the
State.   How many of their American equiv-
alents are in Congress and the Senate?

It has been said — quite falsely — that
Washington made his wife unhappy. A
number of these scandals have a clergyman
for their source; but no more than some
lawyers can kill our ideal of Justice, are some
parsons able to disgust us with Religion.
The various tales have been tracked down

127

to the nothing they started from, even the apparently solid one of the Virginia tombstone bearing a name and the words, "The natural son of Washington." There is no such tombstone, and never was. Most of these forgeries originated during the time of the Conway cabal, when Lee (of Monmouth dishonor), and Gates, and others put their hands to anything that might hurt Washington; but it was themselves that the pitch ultimately defiled. Through Washington's forty years of married life there was constant mutual devotion between his wife and himself, reliance upon him from her, and from him solicitude for her when the war kept them apart, and affection when they were together. While Mr. Lear, his last secretary, and Dr. Craik, his warm friend and physician, were at his death-bed, "fixed in silent grief, Mrs. Washington, who was sitting at the foot of the bed, asked with a firm and collected voice, 'Is he gone?'" Mr. Lear could not

speak but held up his hand as a signal that
he was. "''Tis well,' said she in a plain
voice. 'All is now over. I have no more
trials to pass through. I shall soon follow
him.'" [This is from Lear's account.] And
on the next day, "Mrs. Washington desired
that a door might be made for the Vault,
instead of having it closed up as formerly,
after the body should be deposited, observing,
'That it will soon be necessary to open it
again.' From that day, she moved from
their room to a little room above it, which
had the only window in the house whence
his grave could be seen. There she lived
until she followed him."

Into the quiet of Mount Vernon, some
six years after Washington's marriage, broke
the rumors and rumblings that were to end
in Revolution, and from that time on his
mind was increasingly aroused. We may
perhaps set our finger upon the very day that
saw him waken to resentment against Eng-

land, — *home* as he called her to the last
possible moment, — the 29th of May, 1765,
when the House of Burgesses at Williamsburg
was thrown into debate "most bloody"
(as Jefferson describes it) by certain seven
resolutions moved by an uncouth young
rustic of genius. Patrick Henry had already
severely disconcerted the established leaders
of Virginia by his argument in the "Parsons'
Cause" in December, 1763, when the wrong
side, through him, had won. But on this
occasion, by those resolutions about taxation
offered by this new member, and by his speech
— "if this be treason, make the most of it"
— places were changed, and Peyton Randolph, Richard Bland, George Wythe, and
Edmund Pendleton, sorely against their
judgment and liking at first, followed the lead
of Patrick Henry into the Revolution. We
can see the progress of Washington's mind
through the next ten years in brief fragments
of his letters — those ten years that saw

130

Franklin before Parliament, the Boston "massacre" (a large name to have given it), the tea tax (after which Washington went without all taxed articles), the Burgesses' many dissensions with the royal governors, the Boston Tea Party, the Boston Port Bill, the Continental Congress to which he rode as delegate with Pendleton and Henry, and at length the outbreak of war: —

"The Stamp Act . . . engrosses . . . conversation . . . many luxuries . . . can well be dispensed with . . . where, then, is the utility of these restrictions? . . . Great Britian will be satisfied with nothing less than the deprivation of American freedom. . . . Yet arms . . . should be the last resource. . . . Is it against the duty of three pence per pound on tea? . . . No, it is the right only . . . Great Britian hath no more right to put . . . hands into my pocket . . . than I have to put hands into yours. . . . I could wish, I own, that the dispute had been left to posterity. . . . If it can not be arrested . . . more blood will be spilled . . . than history has ever yet furnished instances of in North America. . . . I am well satisfied that no such thing is desired by any thinking man in all North America . . . that it is the ardent wish . . . that peace . . . upon constitutional grounds, may be restored. . . . I can solemnly declare to you, that, for a year or two past, there has been scarce a moment, that I could properly call my own, that with my own business, my present ward's, my mother's, Colonel Colville's, Mrs. Sawyer's, Colonel Fairfax's, Colonel Monro's, and . . . my brother Augustine's concerns . . . together with the share I take in public affairs . . . I have really been deprived of every kind of enjoyment."

At the time he rides to the Continental Congress, an account of him is given by a fellow Virginian among a number of pithy descriptions: Of Randolph, "a venerable

132

man . . . an honest man . . . a true Roman spirit;" of Bland, "a wary, old, experienced veteran . . . has something of the look of old musty parchments, which he handleth and studieth much;" of Henry, "in religious matters a saint; but the very devil in politics; a son of thunder;" and of Washington, "a soldier, — a warrior; he is a modest man; sensible; speaks little; in action cool, like a bishop at his prayers."

Yes, he spoke little, and his quiet, with so much wisdom behind his rare words, must have been a balm in that Babel of bickering and jealousy. The "Fathers" did not sit in an exalted harmony of patriotism and knee-breeches, as they have been too often pictured to us; it was with them a cat-and-dog affair, not seldom, as it is with us; this it is better to know plainly, to save us from that shallow error of lamenting that in every respect we have fallen away from them. At any one moment of the world, there are thousands of times more fools alive than wise men, but in spite of this, we fall heirs to what the wise men accomplished, while the fools' work is mostly perishable in the long run.

The journal of the Continental Congress discloses, in spite of its cautious meagreness, that the Fathers were inharmonious. "Tuesday, Sep. 6, 1774 . . . *Resolved*, That in determining questions in this Congress, each Colony or Province shall have one Vote. — The Congress not being possess'd of . . . materials for ascertaining the importance of each Colony." "The difficulty to be met was raised by Virginia, who claimed a prominence that the delegates from other Colonies were unwilling to concede." [Connecticut delegates to Governor Trumbull, Oct. 10, 1774.] We have further, and more piquant, elucidations from the diary of John Adams, whose nerves were frequently jangled by his colleagues. "Oct. 24, Monday. In Congress, nibbling and quibbling as usual.

There is no greater mortification than to sit with half a dozen wits deliberating upon a petition, address, or memorial. These great wits, these subtle critics, these refined geniuses, these learned lawyers, these wise statesmen, are so fond of showing their parts and powers, as to make their consultations very tedious." Thus he frets, in wholesale, and thus on another day he breaks out concerning one of the delegates from South Carolina: "a perfect Bob-o-Lincoln, a swallow, a sparrow, a peacock; excessively vain, excessively weak, and excessively variable and unsteady, jejune, inane, and puerile." We need not believe that the gentleman over whom John Adams pours so many epithets was quite as bad as all that, when we look in the face those extraordinary and peevish words he wrote many years later about George Washington: "I will be bolder still, Mr. Taylor. Would Washington have ever been commander of the revolutionary army or president of the United States, if he had not married the rich widow of Mr. Custis?" He also laid Jefferson's eminence to his wife's dollars. Was it because of the rich widow of Mr. Custis that John Adams had himself stood on the floor of Congress and nominated Washington for commander-in-chief? The true reasons shall presently be made clear. It may be gathered from the foregoing fragments from the journal of the Continental Congress and Adams's diary, that, beyond their common enemy, England, North and South had little in common; Virginia is claiming a prominence that angers New England, Massachusetts (in the voice of John Adams) is calling South Carolina a peacock, and here is the feeling of Washington, soon after reaching Cambridge, as to the Massachusetts troops: "I dare say the men would fight very well (if properly officered) although they are an exceeding dirty and nasty people." What do we hear in all these voices but the preluding strains of that Civil War waiting ahead of them, almost ninety years down the road of time? But on happier days, the Fathers could sit in harmony, and perhaps we may deem this a preluding strain of the ultimate, sorely-tested Union: "Sep. 18, 1774. *Resolved unanimously.* That this assembly feels deeply the suffering of their countrymen in the Massachusetts Bay. . . ." As to which, John Adams, in his nobler mood: "This was one of the happiest days of my life. . . . I saw the tears gush into the eyes of the old, grave, pacific Quakers of Pennsylvania."

There was now no escape from war; Washington went to Mount Vernon to prepare for it and was there until called back to Congress in Philadelphia. Again in his own words we read his mind, and the quick march of events:—

"(January, 1775.) I had like to have forgot to express my entire approbation of

137

the laudable pursuit you are engaged in, of
training an independent company. . . . A
great number of very good companies . . .
are now in excellent training; the people
being resolved, altho' they wish for nothing
more ardently than . . . reconciliation . . .
not to purchase it at the expense of their
liberty. . . .

"General Gage acknowledges . . . his men
made a very precipitate retreat from Concord.
. . . A brother's sword has been sheathed in
a brother's heart . . . and the peaceful plains
of America are either to be drenched with
blood, or inhabited by slaves. . . .

"(June 16, 1775.) Mr. President: Though
I am truly sensitive of the high honor done
me in this appointment, yet I feel great
distress from a consciousness that my abilities
. . . may not be equal to the . . . trust. . . .
As to pay, Sir . . . as no pecuniary consideration could have prompted me to accept
this . . . I do not wish to make any profit

138

from it. I will keep an exact account of my
expenses . . . and that is all I desire." (It
was all he desired when he became President, also.) 18 June, 1775. "My dearest,
I am now set down to write you on a subject
which fills me with inexpressible concern."
. . . 19 June, 1775 (To his brother): "Dear
Jack, — I have been called upon by the
unanimous voice of the colonies to take the
command of the continental army. . . ."
19 June, 1775. "Dear Sir, I am now Im-
barked on a tempestuous ocean, from whence
perhaps no friendly harbor is to be found."

In spite of John Hancock's aspirations,
his Massachusetts colleague, John Adams,
had nominated the Virginian, triumphing
over his frequent provincial narrowness with
a generous and patriotic breadth. Since
Braddock's defeat, Washington had been the
greatest military figure in the colonies, his
presence in Philadelphia had commanded
new respect from those gathered there, and

139

no other American had the authority and
the following to override all jealousies and
unite all views. John Adams saw this,
and certainly of him it may be said that the
good he did lives after him, while it is rather
the evil that is interred with his bones. —
When Washington heard his name come from
Adams's lips, he took himself hastily out of
the room; indeed, tradition says that he
ran!

Since that May day in Williamsburg,
1759, when he blushed and took his seat in
the House of Burgesses, sixteen years had
gone over his head. He was now forty-three,
his figure not more filled out than formerly —
it never became so — and he was as straight
and strong as ever. But although his plantation, and riding out before sunrise, and
hauling the seine, duck shooting, fox-hunting,
the oyster man, — all these had kept his
health vigorous and his muscles trained,
his eyes had looked upon approaching storm,

his mind had been hot over the mother country's attack on the core of her child's liberty ("every act of authority of one man over another for which there is not absolute necessity is tyrannical," as Beccaria had put it), and his heart was sore night and day at the thought of breaking with that mother country. As he was leaving Philadelphia for Boston, came the news of Bunker Hill, whereat he asked instantly, had the militia behaved itself? "The liberties of the country are safe!" he exclaimed, on learning of the men's brave conduct. He was a true prophet, but much lay between that word and the goal; we may be sure that his serenity of countenance, of which so many have spoken, was a very grave serenity on the 2d of July, 1775. As the guns of Cambridge thundered for the arriving commander-in-chief, whatever the bows he made to the admiring ladies who looked on, such bows were something of a mask to his preoccupations, when

141

he saw the ragged, gaunt, ill-disciplined troops, and remembered that there had been a total of four barrels of powder in New York when he passed through that city on his way to this army. He took command the next day.

V. THE COMMANDER

Washington and Lafayette at Valley Forge

V

From Napoleon's sneer at this war, which Washington now headed till December, 1783, to Lafayette's gallant and true retort to it, our Revolution has borne every grade of epithet, kind and unkind — as, a war of outposts, a war of skirmishes, a war of retreats, a war of observation. The last is as just a summary of so miscellaneous and outspread a story as could well be hit on; but what matters any name for a fact so portentous in human history? As a war, its real military aspect is slowly emerging from the myth of uninterrupted patriotism and glory, universally taught to school children; its political hue is still thickly painted and varnished over by our writers. How many Americans know, for instance,

that England was at first extremely lenient
to us? fought us (until 1778) with one hand
in a glove, and an olive branch in the other?
had any wish rather than to crush us; had no
wish save to argue us back into the fold,
and enforce argument with an occasional
victory not followed up? that in our counsels,
the determination to be deaf to such argument was not at all times unswerving? and
that had England once consented to keep
the hands of Parliament off us, it is more
than possible we should have agreed to remain "within the empire" on those terms?
How many know the English politics that
lay behind Howe's conduct after the battles
of Long Island, Brandywine, and German-
town — lay behind his whole easy-going
sojourn in this country? Such acts as the
burning of Falmouth (now Portland) and of
Norfolk had not the sanction either of
his policy or Lord North's; but they made,
in Washington's phrase, "fiery arguments"

to sustain our cause. For any American Seven

historian to speak the truth on these matters
is a very recent phenomenon, their common
design having been to leave out any facts
which spoil the political picture of the Revolution they chose to paint for our edification:
a ferocious, blood-shot tyrant on the one side,
and on the other a compact band of "Fathers,"
down-trodden and martyred, yet with im-
peccable linen and bland legs. A wrong
conception even of the Declaration of Independence as Jefferson's original invention
still prevails; Jefferson merely drafted the
document, expressing ideas well established in
the contemporary air. Let us suppose that
some leader of our own time were to write:
"Three dangers to-day threaten the United
States, any one of which could be fatal: unscrupulous Capital, destroying man's liberty to com-
pete; unscrupulous Labor, destroying man's
liberty to work; and undesirable Immigration,
in which four years of naturalization are not

147

going to counteract four hundred years of heredity. Unless the people check all of these, American liberty will become extinct;" — if some one were to write a new Declaration of Independence, containing such sentences, he could not claim originality for them; he would be merely stating ideas that are among us everywhere. This is what Jefferson did, writing his sentences loosely, because the ideas they expressed were so familiar as to render exact definitions needless. Mr. Sydney George Fisher throws all these new lights upon the Revolution, which may perhaps (in its physical aspect) be likened to the gradual wanderings of a half-starved, half-naked man from Massachusetts through New York, New Jersey, and Pennsylvania, down to the Virginia peninsula, where at length he corners his well-fed enemy, and defeats him.

Lucky it is that the day of desperation and distrust did not set in during those first months of Washington's command. From the early moments of his ordering Indian hunting shirts for the army, in order to abolish provincial distinctions, and deciding to besiege Boston, the men knew that a great leader was come to them; this they never forgot through the starvation and nakedness and pennilessness, through the dismal swamp of years through which they followed him. Sometimes misery was too much for them, and they went to their homes in despair, unnerved for reënlistment, but in him they did not cease to believe. With the Boston siege his star rose high; he showed his best powers, and successfully. He read the mind of the foe, he was marvellous in keeping his counsels secret from foe and friend alike, and his moral courage was a sort of tonic in the air. Then his star — and ours — began to sink, helped by the great disappointment, which followed the great hope of Canada's conquest. He had written the

149

noble and sorely troubled Schuyler, whose experiences were proving almost too bitter for him, "We must bear up . . . and make the best of mankind as they are, since we cannot have them as we wish," and to such words Philip Schuyler's generous heart responded. But there was no one to prop Washington thus, as the sky darkened more and more; he had to be his own prop. At Long Island he was outflanked and beaten, the star sank lower, and by the end of 1776 was near setting, when in the deep blackness of Congressional mistrust and military collapse, he risked everything, and the bright light of Trenton and Princeton shone upon the scene. Through all this his own powers showed brilliantly; the English moved out of New Jersey, and our cause had a precious breath of respite, while his masterly strategy got him from the British that title of "the Old Fox." But the star had not really risen yet. The next summer, 1777,

saw what malcontents always called "Fabian
policy"; nothing good happened, and then
on September 10, Brandywine happened
— something bad — another beating from
Howe, much like Long Island, not a well-
managed affair, only to be followed by more
of the same kind, bringing up with German-
town, October 5. It would have now been
black indeed, but in twelve days came that
great turning-point, Burgoyne's surrender
up in the North. At this total failure of a
whole British army, the world began to look
at us with new eyes; but it is hardly unnatural that voices at home said, "No thanks
to Washington." His Brandywine was con-
trasted with Saratoga, for which the specious
Gates got the credit which belonged to Schuyler and others, and then followed the Conway
cabal. This attempt at him behind his
back Washington met in a manner such
that there was presently nothing left of it
or its disgraced leaders; nor did the Valley

Forge winter witness nothing but evil —
rotten as Congress became at this time,
rotten as was the commissariat, rotten as
was everything touched by the political hand.
Important people began to see one or two
important facts: that we had swallowed one
British Army, and that no British Army,
occupy though it might our cities for winter-
quarters and dancing, appeared to be able
to swallow us. There sat Washington at
Valley Forge, cold, hungry, and ragged, no
doubt, — but he sat there, unconquered,
and meanwhile our famous and priceless
friend Steuben had arrived with all his
military knowledge from Frederick the Great,
and was drilling those hungry patriots at
Valley Forge. The result showed at Monmouth Court House, where Clinton, the new
general, got a bad fright and made a narrow
escape, which would have been no escape
at all, but for the treachery of Charles Lee.
The hand which France now took, though with

D'Estaing and his ships it helped us to no victory, helped us most importantly at once in bringing to Europe a knowledge of George Washington. The French officers took news of his greatness and his honorable dealings back with them, and in this way, too, through him our star began to burn brighter. But some dismal swamp was left. We sat for a while at a deadlock with Britain, each side watching the other, and then occurred the treason of Arnold, a dark and heavy catastrophe. Although help from Lafayette and France (where he had gone to stir it up) was really about to come again, it was scarce yet visible, even though Rochambeau was here, and the new year, 1781, began in great darkness. The soldiers had not been paid a penny for twelve months, and man cannot live on patriotism alone. There was mutiny, not unnatural, but of frightful menace, which was met by the politicians with their customary impotence in the face of any great reality. This bred more mutiny, killed quickly by the soldierly Wayne, and in two months the sky brightened, never to cloud so thickly again. Money came from France, and patriotism could at length be fed and clothed; last of all, the sea was made ours by France. This overbore the disaster of Gates at Camden in the preceding August, already somewhat cancelled by his great successor Greene, and by September, Cornwallis was at Yorktown. It was a terrible moment of suspense when the chance seemed that the Count de Grasse, with his ships that gave us the sea during that crucial moment, would sail away before Washington could get down from the Hudson to Virginia; but he waited, and on the 17th of October Cornwallis surrendered. It was two years before Great Britain signed the treaty of peace, but with Yorktown ends the war.

Let us now look at Washington himself

briefly, through these years which have been briefly narrated. Once again we take sentences from his letters covering many months:

"I know the unhappy predicament I stand in; I know that much is expected of me; I know, that without men, without arms, without ammunition, without anything fit for the accommodation of a soldier, little is to be done. . . . My own situation feels so irksome to me at times, that, if I did not consult the public good, more than my own tranquillity, I should long ere this have put everything to the cast of a Dye. . . . Your letter of the 18th descriptive of the jealousies and uneasiness which exist among the Members of Congress is really alarming — if the House is divided, the fabrick must fall. . . . I am sensible a retreating army is encircled with difficulties; that declining an engagement subjects to general reproach, and that the common cause may be affected by the discouragement it may throw over

155

assurances of the disposition of Congress to support him, under his present difficulties and distresses. While I was talking to him I observed him to play with his pen and ink upon several small pieces of paper. One of them by accident fell upon the floor near my feet. I was struck with the inscription upon it. It was 'victory or death.'

"On the following evening I was ordered by General Cadwalader to attend the Militia at Dunk's ferry. An attempt was made to cross the Delaware at that place . . . in order to co-operate with General Washington . . . in an attack upon the Hessians. . . . Floating ice rendered the passage of the river impracticable. . . . The next morning we heard that General Washington had been more successful . . . and taken one thousand Hessians. . . . I found that the countersign of his troops of the surprize of Trenton was, 'Victory or Death.'"

For "near an hour," then, the Philadelphia

158

acquaintance, Dr. Benjamin Rush, had sat with Washington, assuring him of support, and Washington, with his mind full of Trenton that was to happen in thirty-six hours, had sat listening (or perhaps not listening much) and scrawling on little scraps of paper. Was "victory or death" upon all of them, or was he writing various countersigns to see how they looked? At all events, there in the three words is his secret mind before Trenton, while the visitor discoursed about Congress; that pen-scribbling is a very striking instance of how, when the spirit of a man is supremely concentrated, he will often perform trivial, almost unconscious acts. To one familiar with the relations between Washington and Dr. Rush, it may occur that these lay at the bottom of Washington's silence; but this would be an error. Dr. Rush's attack on Dr. Shippen was still to come and to create in Washington the distrust made final by

Dr. Rush's attack on himself in the anonymous letter written to Patrick Henry. All that — the face professions of friendship and the back-hand stab, Henry's loyalty and Washington's deeply moved response to it — was still more than a year off, and Washington would have been silent to any visitor about Trenton, for silence as to his plans was inveterate with him.

His bright letter to Congress the day after Trenton is a marked change from his dark letter the day before it, and in still greater contrast with the whole darkness of his mind disclosed to his brother during that black December, 1776: "If every nerve is not strained to recruit the new army . . . I think the game is pretty nearly up. . . . However, under a full persuasion of the justice of our cause, I can not entertain an Idea that it will finally sink, tho' it may remain for some time under a cloud."

Von Moltke, whose word may be considered as final authority, called Washington one of the world's very greatest strategists, adding: "No finer movement was ever executed than the retreat across the Jerseys, the return across the Delaware a first time, and then a second, so as to draw out the enemy in a long thin line." Genius usually seeks its element as a duck the water, as Alexander looked for "more worlds to conquer." Washington always looked for Mount Vernon, always went back to his crops and his trees, made war as a public duty only; and his military achievement seems to be the fruit, not so much of military genius, but of those great powers and qualities of firmness, sagacity, observation, and detail, which he showed in every undertaking either of war or peace, and of his invaluable training in the Indian wars.

That constitution, of whose strength he wrote Dinwiddie in the early days, was called

upon to meet demands as heavy as those
upon his mind; — after the defeat on Long
Island, for instance, he was on horseback
during the greater part of forty-eight hours,
and his ability to laugh uproariously sometimes must have been an excellent, if rare,
relief for him. General Putnam provided
one great chance for it during the Boston
winter, while several treacheries were being
unearthed. Of one of these they found the
missing link at quite a serious crisis, when the
hiding of our lack of powder was near being
ruined by spies. The missing link turned
out to be a large fat woman, and so trium-
phant and eager was large fat Putnam to
bring her quickly to headquarters, that he
clapped her a-straddle in front of him on
his horse. Washington, looking out of an
upper window, saw this sight approaching,
— an important Puritan General apparently
bearing the spoils of war brazenly before all
eyes — and it is said that he was entirely

overcome, but had mastered his gravity by the time the missing link was deposited in his presence by her assiduous and innocent captor. In the midst of matters so few of which are laughing matters, it would be agreeable to tell and dwell upon every instance of Washington's mirth; but the knowledge must be enough, that he could and did laugh, and that the incident of the fat woman is not the solitary jet of hilarity whose radiance twinkles in that dusk. Of the dearth of powder in one instance an idea may be had by this: owing to a mistake in the report of the Massachusetts committee, instead of four hundred and eighty-five quarter casks of powder, there were only thirty-five half barrels, or not a half a pound to a man. It is recorded that when Washington heard this, he did not utter a word for half an hour. But presently in the midst of more trials we find him quoting poetry, philosophically: "I will not lament or repine . . . because

I am in a great measure a convert to
Mr. Pope's opinion, that whatever is, is
right. . . ."

To quote poetry, or make any literary
allusion, is so rare a thing with him in his
letters, that an instance of it is always a
slight surprise. He writes to young Custis
at his schooling, "For, as Shakespeare says,
'He that robs me of my good name enriches
not himself, but renders me poor indeed,'
or words to that effect." In another place
he serves himself of Hamlet with "in my
mind's eye." He several times uses "under
the rose," and all these seem natural, save
for their great scarcity. But it is quite
astonishing to come upon "*in petto*," and
one comes upon it only once. He seems
fond of the word "maugre," already archaic
in his day, and one wonders where he got it;
but there is one phrase he uses with such
evident relish, and so repeatedly, that to
omit the instances here would be to lose not

only an interesting little fact of his style, but a sign of something deep in the man. It is at one of the deeply disheartening hours of the war that he writes George Mason from Middlebrook, 27 March, 1779: "I have seen without despondency even for a moment . . . the hours which America have stiled her gloomy ones, but I have beheld no day since the commencement of hostilities that I have thought her liberties in such eminent danger as at present. . . . Why do they not come forth to save their Country? let this voice my dear Sir call upon you — Jefferson and others — do not from a mistaken opin- ion that we are about to set down under our own vine, & our own fig tree, let our hitherto noble struggle end in ignom'y — believe me when I tell you there is danger of it — I have pretty good reasons for thinking that Administration a little while ago had re- solved to give the matter up, and negociate a peace with us upon almost any terms;

165

but I shall be much mistaken if they do not now from the present state of our currency and dissensions & other circumstances push matters to the utmost extremity. . . ." In that ringing appeal, the pet phrase appears for the first time, it would seem. And now, let the others come: —

(To Oliver Wolcott.) ". . . but if ever this happens, it must be under my own vine and fig-tree."

(To David Humphreys.) ". . . but neither came to hand until long after I had left the chair of Government, and was seated in the shade of my own Vine and Figtree."

(To Lafayette.) ". . . With what concerns myself personally, I shall not take up your time further than to add, that I have once more retreated to the shades of my own vine and fig Tree."

(To Mrs. Sarah Fairfax.) "Worn out in a manner by the toils of my past labor, I am again seated under my vine and fig-tree."

(To John Adams.) "It is unnecessary, I hope, for me in that event to express the satisfaction it will give Mrs. Washington and me to see Mrs. Adams and yourself, and company in the shade of our vine and fig-tree."

(To J. Q. Adams.) "I am now as you supposed the case would be when you then wrote, seated under the shade of my Vine and Fig-tree."

We may smile, but what a pathos is in these reiterations! They all belong to his last years at Mount Vernon.

One other locution seems to have pleased him, and of its several appearances we give but one, from a letter to Charles Cotesworth Pinckney: "P.S. — Mr. Lewis and Nelly Custis fulfilled their matrimonial engagement on the 22nd of February. In consequence the former, having relinquished the Lapp of

167

Mars for the sports of Venus, has declined
a Military appointment."

Scattered through his letters during the
period of the Revolution, we come upon
various apologies for real or seeming neglect
in hospitality, or cordiality — for failures,
in short, to show people the attention which
they had the right to expect; in these apologies he mentions, among other things, the
weight of his correspondence. As much as
he could he used secretaries, giving them
memorandums, sketched quickly in his own
handsome hand, with many abbreviations:
"The time of my arrival — The situation of
the Troops — Works — & things in general
— Enemy on Bunkers Hill. . . . Express
gratitude for the rediness wch. the Congress
& diff. Committees have shown to make
everything as convenient and agreeable
as possible. . . ." But of course he could
not use secretaries for everything. His brilliant contemporaries and colleagues not seldom

168

shook their heads solemnly over his writings; but they need not have done so. They did so because his sagacity and moral weight so stood out during these distracting times that such gifted men as Jefferson and Hamilton fell dupe to a very human instinct — they wanted to find something which they could do better than he could, and they picked out his English style. They were quite mistaken. While these collateral fathers of the country could *spell* words better than Washington, *use* words better they could not. No better prose than his was written, when he took time to it. There are periods during the war (and periods afterward) when controlled passion or deep concern causes his language to reach the highest level of expression and dignity. During the Conway Cabal, in his papers public and private the style rises so that it would be hard to find writing to surpass it. Specimens are too long to quote,

169

but they are easy to find in the sixth volume
of his correspondence (edited by Ford),
where the reader may look especially at a
letter to Gates, page 362, and one to Bryan
Fairfax, page 389. For the lesson to political
manners of to-day that it contains, we quote
this fragment from the same volume. "If
General Conway means, by cool receptions,
mentioned in the last paragraph of his letter
of the 31st ultimo, that I did not receive him
in the language of a warm and cordial
friend, I readily confess the charge. I did
not, nor shall I ever, till I am capable of the
arts of dissimulation. These I despise, and
my feelings will not permit me to make
professions of friendship to the man I deem
my enemy, and whose system of conduct
forbids it." Conway was at last run to
earth, and his tendered resignation was
accepted when he did not mean it to be.
This so disconcerted him that he wrote saying
his language had been misconstrued: "I

am an Irishman," he protests, "and learnt Seven
my English in France." This is probably Ages of
our only heritage of pure gayety from the Washington
whole contemptible business, in which certain
professed friends cut so poor a figure, and
Lafayette, Richard Henry Lee, and Patrick
Henry shine so brightly. We close this
brief account of Washington's prose style
with one final sentence to show both his own
modesty on this head, and how needless
such modesty was:—

"When I look back to the length of this
letter, I am so much astonished and frightened
at it myself that I have not the courage to give
it a careful reading for the purpose of cor-
rections. You must, therefore, receive it with
all its imperfections, accompanied with this
assurance, that, though there may be in-
accuracies in the letter, there is not a single
defect in the friendship."

His whole bitterness over the Conway Cabal is contained in one sentence written to

171

Governor Livingston, but omitted from the
second draft of the letter: "With many, it
is a sufficient cause to . . . wish the ruin of
a man, because he has been happy enough to
be the object of *his country's* favor." He
underlined the words himself, and this, with
the subsequent omission of the whole, shows
in a stroke his feelings and his reticence.
We have another graphic instance of character
in two notes written General Howe on the
same day, concerning the shorter of which the
Chevalier de Pontgibaud gives the following
account:—

"The British, occupied in the pleasures
which they found in Philadelphia, allowed
us to pass the winter in tranquillity; they
never spoke of the camp at Valley Forges,
except to joke about it, and we for our part
might almost have forgotten that we were
in the presence of an enemy if we had not
received a chance visitor. We were at table
at headquarters — that is to say in the mill,

which was comfortable enough — one day, when a fine sporting dog, which was evidently lost, came to ask for some dinner. On its collar were the words, *General Howe*. It was the British Commander's dog. It was sent back under a flag of truce, and General Howe replied by a warm letter of thanks to this act of courtesy on the part of his enemy, our general." This was Washington's note to Howe: "General Washington's compliments to General Howe, — does himself the pleasure to return him a dog, which accidentally fell into his hands, and, by the inscription on the collar, appears to belong to General Howe." The official one that was written on the same day, October 6, 1777, concerning depredations attributed to Americans and done by British, contains language severely different, and would give no hint of dogs and flags of truce: Washington the commander, writing to Howe the commander, was one thing; Washington the courteous lover of sport, writing to Howe the owner of a lost dog, was another.

The Chevalier de Pontgibaud errs, as the reader will have perceived, as to the place where this happened, for they were not at Valley Forge so early as October, and it was "near Pennibecker's Mill" — the Chevalier is right about there being a mill, and the fact that at Valley Forge there was also a mill is what probably led to this immaterial confusion. Washington's note proves the accuracy of the story, and the following anecdotes also narrated by de Pontgibaud are as vivid, and may equally be accepted, whether they occurred at "Valley Forges," as he called it, or not exactly there.

"One day we were at dinner at headquarters; an Indian entered the room, walked round the table, and seized a large joint of hot roast beef. We were all much surprised, but General Washington gave orders that he was not to be interfered with, saying laughingly, that it was apparently the dinner hour of this Mutius Scævola of the New World. On another occasion a chief came into the room where our Generals were holding a council of war. Washington, who was tall and very strong, rose, coolly took the Indian by the shoulders, and put him outside the door."

It may be that the degrading dissensions, incompetences, and dishonesties of Congress reached, about the Valley Forge period, a low-water mark that they never surpassed in war time (in peace time later, they did); but however that is, it can scarce too much be insisted that our Revolution was not a sort of flawless architectural fabric, made wholly of colonial pillars and patriotism, but that it had a sordid, squalid back-door and premises, of which Gouverneur Morris writes Washington: "Had our Saviour addressed a Chapter to the Rulers of Mankind . . . I am persuaded his good sense would have dictated this text — be not wise overmuch. . . . The most precious moments pass unheeded away like vulgar Things." Such is a gentle way of putting it; but hearken now to the anything but gentle Washington: —

(To James Warren, 31 March, 1779.) "The measure of iniquity is not yet filled . . . Speculation, Peculation . . . afford . . . glaring instances of its being the interest . . . of too many . . . to continue the war. . . . Shall a few designing men . . . to gratify their own avarice, overset the goodly fabric we have been rearing at the expense of so much time, blood, & treasure? And shall we at last become the victims of our own abominable lust of gain? Forbid it Heaven! Forbid it all & every State in the Union! . . . Our cause is noble. It is the cause of mankind. . . ."

If absolutely nothing from his letters were collected save passages devoted to the political iniquities, such passages would make a volume; so would the passages asking for powder, and so those asking for food and clothing, and a fourth could be filled with his protests against short enlistments, by reason of which his army was constantly dissolving in his hands. A Harvard degree, and a medal from Congress (in one of its more amiable and coherent moods) could not have gone very far to compensate him for what he was enduring.

"General Fry, that wonderful man, has made a most wonderful hand of it. . . . He has drawn three hundred and seventy five dollars, never done one day's duty, scarce been three times out of his home. . . . I have made a pretty good slam among such kind of officers . . . having broke one Colo. and two Captains for cowardly behavior . . . two Captains for drawing more provisions and pay than they had men . . . and one for being absent from his post when the enemy

appeared. . . . Different regiments were
upon the point of cutting each other's throats
for a few standing locusts near their encamp-
ment, to dress their victuals with . . . it
will be very difficult to prevail on them to
remain a moment longer than they choose
themselves. . . . Such a dearth of public
spirit . . . I never saw before . . . and pray
God I may never be witness to again. . . .
The Connecticut troops will be prevailed
upon to stay no longer than their terms. . . .
Could I have forseen what I have, and am
likely to experience, no consideration upon
earth should have induced me to accept this
command . . . but we must bear up . . .
and make the best of mankind as they are,
since we can not have them as we wish."
This last philosophical sentence, it will be
remembered, he wrote his friend General
Schuyler, and it is a thought we come upon
several times. Thus, after blowing off his
just rage, would he reënter the splendid

178

poise of his staying-power. It is exhilarating to find him taking a "good slam" with his muscles also on a certain occasion. He rode into camp suddenly upon a fist fight, begun with mere snow-balling, between some newly arrived Virginians and some New England men. Such a fight was of vital menace to the army, full of northern and southern jealousies. He leaped from his horse, took two Virginians by their throats, and shook them in such fashion, talking the while, that in a very few moments he and they were the only people left in sight.

No excess of investigation (and there can be such a thing) would enable us to put our finger upon the moment of the lowest ebb of Washington's staying-power during this war of rags and starvation. There were several moments of very low ebb; but tradi- tion hands one down from Valley Forge, connected with a white-handled pen-knife, upon which small instrument the fortunes of America would seem during that moment to have hung. Together with a clock, whose hands were stopped by an attending physician in Washington's bedroom as he expired, and which have marked that hour ever since, this white-handled pen-knife is treasured in the Masonic museum at Alexandria, and was given to Washington by his mother when he was about fifteen years old. It will be remembered that, but for her, he would have entered the navy in 1746. His brother Lawrence had obtained for him a midshipman's warrant, but it had gone much further than that; the boy's kit had been carried aboard, and he was himself on the point of following it, when a messenger from his mother overtook him, and brought him her final word, so imploring, or so peremptory — tradition says not which — that he abandoned his project, and went home — back to more school and mathematics, as

has been related early in these pages. In
the next order for supplies that his mother
sent to England, she asked for a "good pen-
knife." This, when it came, she gave to the
boy in token of his recent signal submission
to her, adding, "Always obey your superiors." He carried the token all his life, and
to some of his intimates he from time to time
explained its significance. One day at Valley
Forge, when the more than half-naked men
had eaten no meat for many days, and when
Congress had failed once more to provide,
or even to suggest any way for getting, food
and clothes, the ebb was reached, and Washington wrote his resignation as commander-
in-chief of the army. Among the generals
sitting in council, Henry Knox spoke out,
reminding him of the pen-knife, and upon
Washington's asking what that had to do with
it, he said: "You were always to obey your
superiors. You were commanded to lead
this army. No one has commanded you to

181

cease leading it." Washington paused, and
then answered, "There is something in that.
I will think it over." Half an hour later, he
tore his resignation to pieces.

The rumor of what he said and what he did
through all these hours of struggle and desperation, spread wide and far from the centre
of them, spread across the seas, spread to all
distant corners of travel, and the blunt remark
of a Scotchman in Key West bears witness to
what was thought of him by enemies of his
cause. News had come that Washington was
captured, and the Scot was sorry to hear of this,
"for he is too gude a mon to be hangit," he
said, feeling sure this would be the prisoner's
fate. His renown rose to a new height in
that passage of diplomacy that he had with
Lord Howe over the manner in which he
should be styled in letters by the British
commander; after he had sent back a com-
munication addressed "To George Washington Esqre," and a second, where the point was

still dodged, "To George Washington Esqre. &c. &c. &c.," Congress thanked him for thus asserting his dignity, and further resolved that they "have such entire confidence in his judgment . . . they will give him no particular directions." American dignity is not invariably so well guarded by its soldiers, or understood by its civilians. As for the "entire confidence" of Congress, that short-winded affair soon gave out — it spent its time in giving out and reviving; — presently this "entire confidence" was near shifting to Gates, and soon after Gates had blown over came what may have been the heaviest blow, personally, that Washington sustained — Arnold's treason. About this, when he learned it, Washington remarked, simply and quietly: "Whom can we trust now?" Arnold had been a gallant fighter, in fact, a brilliant fighter, and Washington and others (John Adams, for instance) were of opinion that his services had met poor recognition;

Seven Ages of Washington

183

VI. THE PRESIDENT

VI

HE seems to have counted himself now a man whose hard work was done, whose rest was come, a private man, for whom his vine and fig-tree were at last in store; he seems not in the least to have suspected that the new country had further need of him, and he turned his face with relief to Mount Vernon. The war had used his body hard; indeed, his accidental allusion, in a very dangerous moment for him and the country, to his impaired eyesight had saved the critical situation. Between Yorktown and the signing of the peace, the much-enduring army thought it was time for at least a little pay, but Congress, no longer quite so frightened as in the days when it had fled from the enemy's approach, preached sermons of resignation, and suggested that the men placed too high a value upon mere leaving their homes and giving their lives.   It was an incautious hour to choose for so pious a lecture; to the men's angry minds it occurred that there were not many steps to march between themselves and the control of the Government, and they talked of their beloved leader as Dictator. Washington's words quickly burst such a bubble — but this did not stop the mutinous spirit, and Congress, terrified once again by an army, once again had none save Washington to look to for the safety of its skin.   It was a last chance for the intriguing Gates to rise from the discredit of his defeat at Camden, and he played it to the limit. His underhand counsels to the men that their cause was just (which it most assuredly was) and that they must demand their rights, led them to open sedition, and there was Washington where Gates wished him to be, of necessity protecting the Government which was in the wrong, and opposing the men who loved him, and who knew the Government was wrong. There was an hour set for him to meet them, and silence, instead of shouts, was their greeting to him. He had a written address prepared, but on rising to begin it, the text was dim to his eyes, and as he felt for his glasses in that moment during which his own influence and perhaps the country's fate trembled, he spoke simply to the gathered and sullen soldiers the first words that came to him: "I have not only grown gray but blind in your service." By this unpremeditated touch of nature the whole trouble was melted away, the formal address was needless, tears came to the men's cheeks, and they were willing to be patient for their leader's sake.

To Mount Vernon, then, he turned with his gray hairs and weakened sight, reaching there on Christmas eve, "to spend the remainder of my days," he wrote, "in cultivating the affections of good men, and in the practice of the domestic virtues. . . . A glass of wine and a bit of mutton are always ready . . . those who expect more will be disappointed." He presently revisited the trails of his youth, the backwoods, returning thence to the pastoral home existence that he supposed he was now free to enjoy. His daily rising was before the light, his correspondence done by the half-past seven breakfast, after which he rode over his fields until the half-past two dinner; this was followed by writing or by whist until dark. A guest speaks of his agreeableness, his delighting in anecdotes and adventures, silent upon all personal exploits; but Miss Custis saw another side, and described him as being constantly thoughtful and silent, with *lips moving*. Nothing said about him by any one at any time so conveys his inward isolation — inevitable consequence of a great man's moral and mental load — as this report of the moving lips. The money Congress now offered as reward for his services he declined, although his fortune was shrunk and his estate in dilapidation from the war. He speaks picturesquely of returning to find his buildings suffering from many wounds, and here is one of several allusions to straitened circumstances:—

". . . the bonds which were due to me before the Revolution, were discharged during the progress of it — with a few exceptions in depreciated paper (in some instances as low as a shilling in the pound). . . . Such has been the management of my Estate . . . as scarcely to support itself. . . . To keep myself out of debt I have found it expedient now and then to sell Lands. . . ." But, without dwelling further upon his business sense, it is enough to add that he so redeemed his fortune from its serious injuries as to die the second richest man in America. His consummate insight regarding the western

future of the country led him to buy lands
along all the great rivers, from the Mohawk
to the Kanawha, that he foresaw must be
the highways of travel and commerce; in
some cases such lands cost him five pounds
the hundred acres and were sold for five
pounds the acre. Yet his many directions
as to buying and selling show him to have
been far above "sharp practice": "Major
Harrison must be sensible that no one can be
better acquainted with the land than I am;
it would be unnecessary therefore (if he has
any inclination to sell it) to ask a price which
it will not bear; but if he is disposed to take
a reasonable price, and will act the part of a
frank and candid man in fixing it, I would
not have you higgle (which I dislike) in
making a bargain." Such were his methods,
and his fortune came by no means like so
many of those built upon dishonor at the
present day, but as the fair result of superior
sagacity and application. "Land rich," how-

198

ever, as he died, he often lived "land poor," and with income obliterated for a season in consequence of patriotic neglect to watch his own affairs while attending to the affairs of the nation; yet his need of ready money did not check his aid to others in need — the wife of Lafayette, for example, to whom he sent two hundred guineas at once on learning of her husband's imprisonment, or the sufferers from pestilence in Philadelphia to whom he offered assistance through Bishop White, "without ostentation or mention of my name," as he requests the bishop. Nor was it his fashion, as the mode is now, to put on the mask of a benefactor and thus disguised to label colleges and libraries with his own name, thus really leaving his money to himself. His gifts to education were gifts, and not advertisements or obituaries.

Intercolonial jealousies were, as we have seen, in full blossom already by 1776, and now they ripened quickly to full fruit. The common enemy gone, everybody had full time to fall upon his neighbor, and he did so, until they were all nearer to destroying their new country than King George had been; a republic is its own worst enemy, and we showed this then as we show it to-day. Washington would have despised the view expressed by a lesser public servant: "I had rather let the old ship sink, than keep pumping at her all the while;" therefore he tasted but little of his vine and fig-tree, and soon returned to the ship and the pumping. Lafayette, on December 30, 1777, had written to him: "Take away for an instant that modest diffidence of yourself . . . you would see very plainly that if you were lost to America, there is nobody who could keep the army and the revolution for six months. There are open dissensions in congress, parties who hate one another as much as the common enemy." If Washington's modesty forbade his believing this, the quarrelling factions knew it to be true; cat and dog came running to him, and soon he was presiding over the Constitutional Convention.

And now is the time to speak of the third cardinal influence in his life. It rests not on a level with the others, coming upon Washington in the full high-noon of his growth; but in clearing and shaping his mind about what foundations our new government should rest on, and how these should be laid, its importance is unique. The other two were influences upon *character*, the rules of civility and the friendship of Fairfax; the third and last is Alexander Hamilton. Of him, during the war, we have this first glimpse recorded: —

"I noticed a youth, a mere stripling, small, slender, almost delicate in frame, marching beside a piece of artillery with a cocked hat pulled down over his eyes, apparently lost in thought, with his hand resting on the cannon, and every now and then patting it as he mused, as if it were a favourite

horse or a pet plaything." This was Hamilton, not quite twenty years old. Washington, too, caught sight of him at about this
time, noticing (amidst some disastrous hours
of fighting) how skilfully some earthworks
were going forward under the direction of a
young captain of artillery. He sent for the
young man, whose discourse so struck him,
that presently (March 1, 1777) he made him
aide-de-camp with the rank of lieutenant
colonel, and next the young man, now twenty,
was conducting much of the correspondence
of the older man, now fifty-five. Nick-named
"the little lion" by a colleague, Hamilton
was soon "my boy" to Washington. The
boy was already famous through some
pamphlets, and what war did for the disci-
pline and development of his genius — for
genius he had such as none other — must have
been priceless to him, and so to us. What
his genius did for Washington was equally
inestimable. The coming together of these

two, the seasoned, sagacious intelligence, and the winged, fiery intellect, may be likened to some beneficent chemical union between acid and alkali, producing as it did the very salt of constructive common sense. If this had not, on the whole, prevailed during the stormy years that were now to set in, we should have been to-day but another nest of hornet republics, like the hemisphere to the south of us, or else swallowed up by a foreign power. Among the sundry passages that Washington wrote about the case of the new country, we take two: —

(1785.) "The war . . . has terminated most advantageously for America, and a fair field is presented to our view; but I confess to you freely, my dear Sir, that I do not think we possess wisdom or justice enough to cultivate it properly. Illiberality, jealousy, and local policy mix too much in all our public councils for the good government of the Union. . . . The confederation appears

. . . little more than a shadow . . . and Congress a nugatory body. . . . To me . . . it is one of the most extraordinary things in nature, that we should confederate as a nation, and yet be afraid to give the rulers of that nation who are the creatures of our making, appointed for a limited and short duration, and who are amenable for every action . . . sufficient powers to order and direct the affairs of the same. . . . By such policy . . . we are descending into the vale of confusion and darkness. That we have it in our power to become one of the most respectable nations upon earth, admits, in my humble opinion, of no doubt, if we would but pursue a wise, just, and liberal policy towards one another, and keep good faith with the rest of the world." (This sentence about "good faith" arose from his seeing the populist instinct not to pay your creditors rapidly growing.) Later, 1787: "I almost despair of seeing a favourable issue to the proceedings of our convention, and do therefore repent having had any agency in the business. The men who oppose a strong and energetic government, are in my opinion narrow-minded politicians. . . . The apprehension expressed by them, that the *people* will not accede to the form proposed, is the *ostensible*, not the *real* cause of opposition. . . . I am sorry you went away. I wish you were back." (This is to Hamilton.)

We find more angry and more despondent words than these in his letters at this time, but what has been quoted clearly shows his thoughts and feelings; presently the Constitution was adopted, and next, on April 14, 1789, a deputation from Congress waited on him at Mount Vernon, and formally announced that he was unanimously elected first President of the United States. "I wish," he replied, "that there may not be reason for regretting the choice." To Knox, his war comrade, he wrote: "In confidence,

I tell *you* . . . that my movement to the chair of Government will be accompanied by feelings not unlike those of a culprit who is going to the place of his execution."

Vine and fig-tree were left behind in this spirit, in which there is nowhere to be found any sign of elation, but only personal regret and unwillingness, and a solemn dedication of self to the new needs of the country. The greeting he met, the universal shout of loyalty, when he stepped forth upon the balcony at his inauguration, caused him to falter and sit down, and this brought a silence as intense and universal as the cheering had been. Thus he took his oath, and then turned to enter a maze of troubles of every size and shape, from the petty follies about the etiquette of his receptions to the question how the American people could be persuaded to pay their debts both domestic and foreign. There was scarce a meanness too small or a blindness too great for some of the chief citizens of that day; and everything was brought to him, or if it was not brought, the responsibility of dealing with it fell upon him nevertheless, and he got the blame whenever any one was not pleased. "We have probably had too good an opinion of human nature in forming our confederation," he had written a little while before, and what he now began to experience was not likely to disabuse him of this opinion, but only to send him back to the same philosophy he had once preached to General Schuyler to "make the best of mankind as they are, since we can not have them as we wish." Etiquette, then (as to which Hamilton, Adams, and Jefferson all differed), had to be established, just how much and how little there should be, and this practical question was complicated not only by differences of opinion, but by not a little false and ridiculous gossip. Some of this is eagerly set down by Jefferson in his book of malice that he called

207

Anas, wherein he has written himself down a character to which his worst enemy could scarce add a syllable. He describes Washington and Mrs. Washington as sitting on a sort of throne during a ball, at which, as a matter of fact, they were on the floor dancing during the whole evening. Indian troubles, secretly fomented by the English, harassed our frontier, and a great disaster was suffered, the news of which caused one of those outbreaks of violent emotion to which Washington was subject. His general health showed signs of the worries he lived daily in, among which the greatest, possibly, was the problem of finance. The doctrine of not paying your debts was offered in various sugar-coated forms of rhetoric as a *principle* that should form part of our national policy. Taxation was felt to be an insult to American freedom, and a strong party came into existence whose aim may be fairly said to have been to resolve our Republic into a "society for the avoidance of personal obligations" — to quote the admirable words of Mr. Oliver in his study of Alexander Hamilton. "According to the practice of demagogy," this writer continues, "the doctrine of repudiation was . . . raised to a higher moral plane. In the twilight of words and phrases the seductive idea, like a lady of doubtful virtue and waning beauty, was arranged in a charitable and becoming shadow. . . ." Thomas Jefferson favored all these things; he worked out one of his ingenious quackeries to show the iniquity of creating a national debt. We had no moral right to make a loan that our children must pay; he produced arithmetic to show that nineteen years is the length of a generation, and he advocated that any debt still unpaid after nineteen years should be extinguished. It may be imagined how attractive such a scheme would be to a "society for the avoidance of personal obligations," and how dear to the hearts of "the

people" Jefferson thus made himself; it
may also be imagined with what heartiness
Holland, or any other country, would have
responded to our application for money,
if such doctrines had prevailed. Shea's
Rebellion — one of our paper-money episodes
of insanity, and at core a local phase of repudiation — had a few years earlier revealed
the ideas of the society for the avoidance of
personal obligation, and for this demonstra-
tion Jefferson had nothing but praise. "God
forbid," he said, "that we should be twenty
years without a rebellion. . . . The tree
of liberty must be refreshed from time to
time with the blood of patriots and tyrants.
It is its natural manure." From this sprightly
and vivacious doctrine he excepted himself;
when Tarleton and his raiders came too near
the Virginia legislature, he fled with a prompt-
ness that showed conclusively he had no intention his own blood should refresh the tree
of liberty. The still more comprehensive

doctrine, that if any man happened to dislike any law, it was his American perquisite
and sacred right to break such law, was
another of the menacing undercurrents during Washington's first term, and during his
second it broke out in the Whiskey Insur-
rection. It was deemed by true Jeffer-
sonians, such as Edmund Randolph, a
despotic outrage upon liberty that troops
should be sent to enforce order and obedience
to the law. These are the "principles"
that we have inherited from Thomas Jefferson — if it can be said that he had any fixed
principles — and it is no wonder that he
remains a popular idol; the real wonder is,
that Washington, who threw his whole force
against such principles, and with Hamilton's
help largely defeated them, should remain
a popular idol too. It is most natural that
Hamilton, the greatest benefactor our young
country knew, except Washington, should have
no popularity whatever, although his great-

211

or deeper gratitude; but if his political co-
herence, his constructive statesmanship, is
examined, it crumbles away, leaving nothing but a faith in mankind amid a cloud of
dust.

Worry over the mischief made, and the
more mischief attempted, by those who
corresponded in that day to the "green-
backers," the "farmers' alliance," and the
"populists" of later days, impaired Washington's health, and also fatigued and dis-
enchanted him in his ceaseless effort to set
the infant Republic on its legs. The infant
Republic struggled tooth and nail against
this; in fact, toward every measure adopted
for its soundness and permanence, the infant
Republic may be likened in its conduct to an
ill-conditioned, squalling brat, disgusting all
save its most patient guardians. Washington would have been very glad to be free of
the whole business; but the brat, genuinely
scared lest the parent whom it had been

biting and scratching should abandon it to its own devices, clung to him, not in gratitude, but in terror.   Even Jefferson, who had been opposed to the Administration's policy, and, though a member of the cabinet, was encouraging newspaper attacks upon it — if he did not actually dictate many of the articles himself — even Jefferson wished Washington to stay.   Jefferson's most useful trait, perhaps, was a power to drop all his theories in the face of a crisis, and do the practical thing. "North and South will hang together if they have you to hang on," he said; and Washington stayed — but here is how he felt:—

"To say I feel pleasure from the prospect of commencing another tour of duty would be a departure from truth; for, however it might savor of affectation in the opinion of the world (who, by the by, can only guess at my sentiments, as it never has been troubled with them), my particular and confidential

express a sentiment respecting the fitness or
unfitness of any candidate for representation.
. . . The exercise of an influence would be
highly improper; as the people ought to be
entirely at liberty to chuse whom they pleased
to represent them in Congress." But this
highmindedness was lost upon the screaming
infant Republic, feverish with that disease
not yet exterminated, and always fatal if
not kept in check, the disease of plebiscitis.
Sickened by the treatment he received,
Washington speaks without reserve, once, to
Jefferson: ". . . nor did I believe until lately
. . . that, while I was using my utmost exer-
tions to establish a national character of our
own, independent, as far as our obligations
and justice would permit, of every nation of
the earth, . . . every act of my administration would be tortured . . . and that too in
such exaggerated and indecent terms as could
scarcely be applied to a Nero, a notorious
defaulter, or even to a common pickpocket."

A delirious dread of Washington's becoming king — he pronounced it insane himself to Jefferson, who feared, or made believe to fear it — was continually fomented by the papers, of which he took no public notice; but his letters are full of the evidences of his feeling. "In a word," he writes Edmund Randolph before the scandal of the French minister had ended their relations, "if the government and the offices of it are to be the constant theme for newspaper abuse, and this too without condescending to investigate the motives or the facts, it will be impossible, I conceive, for any man living to manage the helm or to keep the machine together."

It is curious to read those newspapers of the 1790's and see how much time has moderated the violence of words, though not at all the poison of slander and sensation. It could not be printed to-day that "the eldest son of Satan, Albert Gallatin, arrived in town yesterday afternoon." They dared not go so far with Washington's name, but they spent much ingenuity upon him. In a sort of burlesque dictionary, published in Freneau's *Gazette*, Philadelphia, 24 April, 1793, we find: "*Great man*. Excellent judge of horse-flesh." And again, "Valerius" (or "Brutus" or "Publius") writes: "If the *form* of monarchy was exalted among us, a national love of liberty would rally all around the standard of opposition, except the minions of the idol." Once more: "The temple of Liberty, like that of Vesta, should never be without a centinel. . . . Were I to see public servants excluding private citizens from their tables, I should not hesitate to sound the alarm." We may wonder, if every American had the right to dine with his President, how long the cook would stay. Let us see what the hapless public servant had to say about this last accusation: "Between the hours of three

220

and four every Tuesday, I am prepared to
receive. . . . Gentlemen, often in great num-
bers, come and go, chat with each other,
and act as they please. . . . Similar . . .
are the visits every Friday afternoon to Mrs.
Washington, where I always am. — These —
and a dinner once a week to as many as my
table will hold — are as much, if not more,
than I am able to undergo; for I have already had, within less than a year, two severe
attacks — the last one worse than the first.
A third, more than probably, will put me to
sleep with my fathers." To this, let the
following, with its unconscious pathos and
irony be appended. "31st July, 1797. Dear
Sir: I am alone at *present* . . . unless
some one pops in unexpectedly, Mrs. Washington and myself will do what I believe has
not been done in the last twenty years by
us — that is to set down to dinner by ourselves."

During these first momentous years, two

forces — the perennial forces of our Commonwealth, the Federal power and the State power — were to be apportioned and proportioned, and between these Washington's strength was continually ground. Any event, any question, whether domestic or foreign, set them raging. Had the centrifugal force outbalanced the other, we should have been all tire and no axle; the wheels of the Republic would have sunk in splinters. Those who dreaded on the other hand that we should be all axle and no tire, pushed their dread rather fantastically; but certainly, if the wheels are to stay sound and turning, we need the perpetual, adjusted equilibrium of those two forces; the United States are a federation, each one remaining a whole as regards each of the others, though it be a part as regards the whole. But upon Washington the grinding told, and with the ill consequences to his health came some not surprising signs of increasing irascibility.

222

Several references to violent outbreaks on his part have been made; the news of St. Clair's defeat by the Indians had caused one of these, narrated by the single person in whose presence it occurred. Of another, which took place in the presence of the whole cabinet, Jefferson gives the account. "Knox in a foolish, Incoherent sort of speech introduced the Pasquinade lately printed, called the funeral of George Washington, and James Wilson, King and Judge, &c., where the President was placed on a guillotine. The President was much inflamed, got into one of those passions when he can not command himself, ran on to the personal abuse which had been bestowed on him, defied any man on earth to produce one single act of his since he had been in the government which was not done on the purest motives, that he had never repented but once the having slipped the moment of resigning his office, and that was every moment since, that *by God* he would break any law that displeased you; but we must do these people what justice we can. There was a wide and righteous gratitude to France for what she had done to help our own Revolution, and there was a treaty with her, besides an equally wide and natural hatred of England, with whom France was presently at war. Where these people failed to discriminate was in their inability to see that the France who had helped us, the France of Lafayette and Rochambeau, of Louis XVI, was not the France they wished to befriend in return; *our* France had been pulled down by a mob, and it was not even to its ruins, but to the mob, that American sympathy was directed. Bache's paper of May 25, 1793, expresses the general belief in saying: "The fact will be found to be, that the French understand the principles of a free government — that the English do not." Nothing that Washington did brought him bitterer hate than his stand for neutrality when

226

England went to war with France. The French party here would have rushed this tottering young country into a European strife. Some one from Pittsburgh writes to Freneau's *Gazette:* "Louis Capet has lost his Caput. From my use of a pun, it may seem that I think lightly of his fate. I certainly do." And the same paper later addresses Washington: "Sir . . . The cause of France is the cause of man, and neutrality is desertion. . . . I doubt much whether it is the disposition of the United States to preserve the conduct you enjoin. . . . The American mind is indignant, and needs but to be roused a little to go to war with England and assist France." For a while the volatile Jefferson busily connived at all this, busily befriended the French envoy, the impudent and meddlesome Genêt. We cannot go into the case of the *Little Sarah*, that was fitted out to aid France and sailed away under Jefferson's nose. There

"American mind" felt such sympathy; a France of rivers of blood, in which danced monkeys and assassins. Even the flighty Jefferson's vision of the millennium was troubled during the Reign of Terror, and we find him writing a very mixed metaphor to the effect that "the arm of the people" is "blind to a certain degree." After 1792, France was republic, directorate, consulate, monarchy, and empire, changing its form of government ten times in eighty years. We recall and assemble these familiar facts in order that against their background the reader may more instantly see the value of Washington's neutrality, and the folly of the very powerful and clamorous party who denounced it; but to see these things fully, the newspapers of that day should be read. From the many echoes of doubt and distrust in our stability caused by the resistance to taxation and the sympathy with the French Revolution, we select a few lines

230

written from Congress by the same Jeremiah Smith who became chief justice of New Hampshire: —

"You perceive that we have been, I may say still are, on the edge of a precipice, ready to take a leap into the abyss of confusion. . . . God knows how this ship of ours will sail, when the present pilot quits the helm. If we may judge from present appearances, she will inevitably founder."

From the pilot's own letters we select and place together for the last time some sentences dealing with a few of his problems — many of them still our problems — and showing the man himself after his encounter with them.

"The difference of conduct between the friends and foes of . . . good government, is . . . that the latter are always working like bees to distil their poison; whilst the former, depending often times *too much* and *too long* upon the sense and good disposition of the people to work conviction, neglect

231

mass of citizens in these United States *mean
well*, and I firmly believe they will always
act well whenever they can obtain a right
understanding . . . but in some parts of the
Union, where the sentiments of their delegates and leaders are adverse to the government, and great pains are taken to inculcate
a belief that their rights are assailed and their
liberties endangered, it is not easy to accom-
plish this; especially, as is the case invariably, when the inventors and abettors of
pernicious measures use infinite more industry in disseminating the poison, than the
well-disposed part of the community to fur-
nish the antidote. . . ."

As has been said, he began as a man of no
party, but became inevitably ranged with
the Federalists; his political affinity with
Hamilton, his affection for him — ever warmer
as the years went on — and his modest
recognition of Hamilton's superior gifts in
statesmanship, led him to go to his friend with

every question that he was pondering, even small ones. Adet, the third unsatisfactory envoy from France, had published a letter to the Secretary of State: —

". . . whether the *publication* in the manner it appears is by order of the Directory, or an act of his own, is yet to be learnt. If the first, he has executed a duty only; if the latter, he exceeded it, and is himself responsible for the indignity offered to this Government by such publication, without allowing it time to reply. . . . In either case, should there be in your opinion any difference in my reception and treatment of that Minister in his visits at the public Rooms (I have not seen him yet, nor do not expect to do it before Tuesday next) — and what difference should be made if any?"

To which Hamilton answers: —

"The true rule on this point would be to receive the Minister at your levees with a *dignified reserve,* holding an *exact medium*

between an *offensive coldness* and *cordiality.*
The point is a nice one to be hit, but no one
will know how to do it better than the President."

We dwell not upon his Farewell Address, his own idea and work — though it
benefited by the criticism of Hamilton ; it
needs no mention here; we finish with
a few further examples of his opinions.
"I was in hopes that motives of policy as
well as other good reasons supported by
the direful effects of slavery . . . would
have operated to produce a total pro-
hibition of the importation of slaves. . . .
Were it not that I am principled against
selling negroes . . . I would not in twelve
months from this date be possessed of one,
as a slave. I shall be happily mistaken if
they are not found to be very troublesome
species of property ere many years pass over
our heads. . . . We are *all* the children of
the same country. . . . Our interest . . . is

236

the same. . . . My system . . . has uni- formly been . . . to contemplate the United States as one great whole . . . for sure I am, if this country is preserved in tranquillity twenty years longer, it may bid defiance in a just cause to any power whatever; such in that time will be its population, wealth and resources. . . . [The next regards the Federal City which he had in mind.] I take the liberty of sending you the plan of a new city, situated about the centre of the Union of these States, which is designated for the permanent seat of government. . . . A century hence if this country keeps united (and it is surely its policy and interest to do it) will produce a city, though not so large as London, yet of a magnitude inferior to few others in Europe, on the banks of the Potomac . . . where elegant buildings are erecting and in forwardness for the reception of Congress in the year 1800. . . . [This concerns his third term.] It would be a matter of sore regret to me, if I could believe that a serious thought was turned towards me . . . for, although I have abundant cause to be thankful for the good health with which I am blessed, yet I am not insensible to my declination in other respects. It would be criminal, therefore, in me, although it would be the wish of my countrymen . . . to accept an office . . . which another would discharge with more ability."

This is the person whom they pictured on the guillotine; the author of that Farewell Address more times printed than any American state document; and this is the person of whom the newspaper, Bache's *Aurora*, said upon his retiring from the presidency: "If ever a Nation was debauched by a man, the American Nation has been debauched by Washington."

So much patience of mind seems never to have belonged to any other great public man; to take difficult thoughts, one by one,

and march slowly to their end, and so to
reach conclusions which were impregnable
then, and which time itself has left unassailed,
this was his preëminent quality. Very
different he was from the ingenious, better-
educated Jefferson, whose mind leaped lightly
to attractive generalizations, which the ruth-
less test of actuality finds to be mostly rub-
bish. The two may be styled the hare and
the tortoise of our Independence. One
other great quality comes forth from all
Washington's deeds and words, like a beautiful glow; its lustre seems to shine in every
page that he writes, and in all his dealings with
men, with ideas, with himself; it is the quality
of simplicity. Our fathers had it more than
we of to-day, and it would be well for us if we
could regain it. The Englishman of to-day
is superior to us in it; he has in general,
no matter what his station, a quiet way of
doing and of being, of letting himself alone,
that we in general lack. We cannot seem

239

to let ourselves alone; we must talk when there is nothing to say; we must joke — especially we must joke — when there is no need for it, and when nobody asks to be entertained. This is the nervousness of democracy; we are uncertain if the other man thinks we are "as good" as he is; therefore we must prove that we are, at first sight, by some sort of performance. Such doubt never occurs to the established man, to the man whose case is proven; he is not thinking about what we think of him. So the Indian, so the frontiersman, so the true gentleman, does not live in this restlessness. Nor did Washington; and therefore he moved always in simplicity, that balanced and wholesome ease of the spirit, which when it comes among those who must be showing off from moment to moment, shines like a quiet star upon fireworks.

And how did the man who had been twice President now look? The descriptions of him belonging to this period tell of changes. Less mention is made of his agreeable smile, his cheerful serenity, his pleasant talk; it is his gravity, his reticence, even his melancholy — this is the record. Is it surprising in one who, when reticence was during an angry moment broken, had declared that he would rather be in his grave than in his present situation? If Arnold had added a furrow to his face, there must have been many new ones by this time; but here is one word about himself, written in considerable indignation, that unveils something of the depths he usually concealed: "Whether you have, upon any occasion, expressed yourself in disrespectful terms of me, I know not — it has never been the subject of my enquiry. If nothing impeaching my honor or honesty is said, I care little for the rest. I have pursued one uniform course for threescore years, and am happy in *believing* that the world have thought it a right one — of it's being so, I am so well satisfied myself, that I shall not depart from it by turning either to the right or to the left, until I arrive at the end of my pilgrimage."

An agreeable and graphic account of Washington the President is given in the privately published memoirs of Mr. Charles Biddle, a distinguished Philadelphian of that day: —

"When he was elected President of the United States, he lived during the whole of the time that he was in Philadelphia nearly opposite to me. At that time I saw him almost daily. I frequently attended levees to introduce some friend or acquaintance, and called sometimes with Governor Mifflin. The General always behaved politely to the Governor, but it appeared to me he had not forgotten the Governor's opposition to him during the Revolutionary war. He was a most elegant figure of a man, with so much dignity of manners, that no person whatever

could take any improper liberties with him.
I have heard Mr. Robert Morris, who was
as intimate with him as any man in America,
say that he was the only man in whose presence he felt any awe. You would seldom
see a frown or a smile on his countenance,
his air was serious and reflecting, yet I have
seen him in the theatre laugh heartily. Dr.
Forrest, who laughs a great deal, desired
me one night at the theatre, to look at
General Washington. 'See how he laughs,
by the Lord he must be a gentleman.'
The General was in the next box, and I
believe heard him. He was much more
cheerful when he was retiring from office
of President than I had ever seen him before. Commodore Barry, Major Jackson,
and myself were appointed a Committee
of the Society of Cincinnati to wait upon
him with a copy of an address, and to know
when it would be convenient for the Society
to wait upon him. He received us with great

good humor, and laughing, told us that he
had heard Governor Morris (I believe of
New Jersey) say that when he knew gentlemen were going to call on him with an address,
he sent to beg they would bring an answer.
If this were done to him, he observed that it
would save him a great deal of trouble. He
was in Philadelphia a short time before he
died, and I thought he never looked better
than he did at that time. . . . He was
called the American Fabius, but Fabius was
not equal to George Washington. He suffered Tarentum to be pillaged when it was
traitorously delivered to him, and his opposition and jealousy of Scipio rendered the
Roman unequal to the American hero."

It is upon the day of his release, the day
when public burdens fell from him, and the
vine and fig-tree began to draw near in his
hopes, that we shall take our farewell look
at him. His successor, John Adams, had
finished taking his oath; Washington turned

to leave the assembly, and at this sight, all who could do so crowded from their places to the hall, that they might see the last of him. He passed through their cheering to the street, where in answer he waved his hat, "his countenance radiant with benignity, his grey hairs streaming in the wind." It is from the lips of an eye-witness that Irving gives this account. "The crowd followed him to his door; there, turning round, his countenance assumed a grave and almost melancholy expression, his eyes were bathed in tears, his emotions were too great for utterance, and only by gestures could he indicate his thanks and convey his farewell blessing."

Three years of quiet he lived to see, and then was dead after brief illness, able to ride his horse to within three days of the end, and ready to take the command against France in case of war. He seemed to know his illness was indeed the end, although, during the twenty hours of its progress he let

245

them try what remedies they wished; when at last his friend Dr. Craik sat on his bed, and took his head in his lap, he said with difficulty: "Doctor, I am dying, and have been dying for a long time, but I am not afraid to die."

VII.   IMMORTALITY

his austere fame, and to be here by the fireplace. Here are some of his very books on the shelves, here the stairs he went up and down, here in the hall his swords, and the key of the Bastille that Lafayette sent to him. Upstairs is the room he died in, and the bed; still above this chamber, the little room where Martha Washington lived her last years after his death, with its window looking out upon the tomb where he was first laid. Everything, every object, every corner and step, seems to bring him close, not in the way of speaking of him or breathing of him, as some memorial places seem to speak and breathe their significance; a silence fills these passages and rooms, a particular motionlessness, that is not changed or disturbed by the constant moving back and forth of the visitors. What they do, their voices, their stopping and bending to look at this or that, does not seem to affect, or even to reach, the strange influence that surrounds them. It is an exquisite and friendly serenity which bathes one's sense, that brings him so near, that seems to be charged all through with some meaning or message of beneficence and reassurance, but nothing that could be put into words.

And then, not staying too long in the house, stroll out upon the grounds. Look away to the woods and fields, whence he rode home from hunting with Lord Fairfax, over which his maturer gaze roved as he watched his crops and his fences, and to which his majestic figure came back with pleasure and relief from the burdens and the admiration of the world. Turn into his garden and look at the walls and the walks he planned, the box hedges, the trees, the flower-beds, the great order and the great sweetness everywhere. And among all this, still the visitors are moving, looking, speaking, the men, women, and children from every corner of the country, some plain and rustic enough, some laughing and talking louder than need be, but all drawn here to

"_He that has light within his own clear breast_
May sit i' the centre, and enjoy bright day."

CHRONOLOGY

DATE	EVENTS	AGE
1756	Military mission to New York and Boston . .	24
1758	Ill health. Courtship. March to the Ohio. Resigned commission	26
1759	Jan. 6. Married to Martha Dandridge Custis .	26
1759	May. Took seat in House of Burgesses . .	27
1765	Commissioner for settling the military accounts of the colony	33
1770	Journey to the Ohio and Kenawha rivers . .	38
1774	Member of the Virginia Convention on the points at issue between England and the Colonies . .	42
1774	Sept. Member of the First Continental Congress .	42
1775	May 10. Member of the Second Continental Congress. June 15. Commander-in-chief. July 3. Took command at Cambridge. Siege of Boston	43
1776	Mar. 17. Boston evacuated by British. Aug. 27. Battle of Long Island. Dec. 26. Battle of Trenton. Dec. 27. Invested by Congress with dictatorial powers	44
1777	Jan. 3. Battle of Princeton. Winter quarters at Morristown. Sept. 11. Battle of Brandywine. Oct. 4. Battle of Germantown . . .	44–45
1778	Winter quarters at Valley Forge. Conway Cabal. June 28. Battle of Monmouth Court-house . . . Arrival of d'Estaing. Winter quarters at Middlebrook	45–46
1779	July 16. Capture of Stony Point . . .	47
1780	Arnold's treason	48
1781	Jan. 1. Pennsylvania troops mutiny. Oct. 19. Surrender of Cornwallis at Yorktown . .	49
1782	Threatening sedition of army and talk of dictator .	50
1783	April 19. Peace proclaimed to the army. Nov. 2. His farewell to the army. Dec. 4. His farewell to his generals. Dec. 23. He resigned his commission at Annapolis. Dec. 24. Home to Mount Vernon	51
1784	Journey to the western country	52

DATE	EVENTS	AGE
1787	May 14. Delegate to Constitutional Convention at Philadelphia. President of the Convention	55
1789	President of the United States. Apr. 30. Inaugurated in New York. Journey through Eastern States	57
1791	Journey through Southern States	59
1793	Second time President of United States. The episode of Genêt, minister from France	61
1796	Sept. 17. Farewell address to the people of the United States	64
1797	Home to Mount Vernon. Troubles with France. Preparations for war	65
1798	July 3. Commander-in-chief of the armies of the United States	66
1799	Dec. 14. Died at Mount Vernon	67

BIBLIOGRAPHY

The Writings of George Washington. Collected and Bibliography edited by Worthington Chauncey Ford. Letterpress Edition. G. P. Putnam's Sons. New York. 1893.

The Life of Washington, by Washington Irving. In 8 volumes. G. P. Putnam's Sons. New York. 1855–59.

The True History of the Revolution, by Sydney George Fisher. J. B. Lippincott Co. Philadelphia. 1902.

Alexander Hamilton, by Frederick Scott Oliver. G. P. Putnam's Sons. New York. 1907.

Patrick Henry, by Moses Coit Tyler. Houghton, Mifflin & Company. Boston. 1887.

The True Thomas Jefferson, by William Eleroy Curtis. J. B. Lippincott Co. Philadelphia. 1901.

George Washington's Rules of Civility, by Moncure D. Conway. John W. Lovell Company. New York. 1890.

Life of the Hon. Jeremiah Smith, LL.D., by John H. Morison. Charles C. Little & James Brown. Boston. 1845.

And the memoirs, privately published, of Benjamin Rush and Charles Biddle, together with the files of *Freneau's Gazette* and *Bache's Aurora,* during the terms of Washington's presidency.